Fire Drill

By the same author

FIRE DRILL

Notes on the
Twenty-First Century

JOHN BARNIE

SEREN

Seren is the book imprint of
Poetry Wales Press Ltd.
57 Nolton Street, Bridgend, Wales, CF31 3AE
www.seren-books.com

ISBN 978-1-85411-519-5

A CIP record for this title is available from the British Library.

The publisher acknowledges the financial assistance of the Welsh Books
Council.

Printed in Plantin Light by Short Run Press Ltd

Mixed Sources
Product group from well-managed
forests and other controlled sources
www.fsc.org Cert no. SA-COC-002112
© 1996 Forest Stewardship Council
FSC

CONTENTS

Acknowledgements

The essays in this collection are previously unpublished, with the exception of 'Maps' which first appeared in *Planet,* and 'What the Raven Told the Eagle' which first appeared in *Poetry Wales.*

My thanks to Helle Michelsen for her criticism and to Mick Felton for his care in seeing the book through the press.

In the space of less than 40,000 years, ever more closely packed cultural "revolutions" have taken humanity from the status of a relatively rare large mammal to something more like a geological force.

Richard G. Klein and Blake Edgar, *The Dawn of Human Culture*

Advanced technology has become the ultimate prosthesis. Take away electric power from a tribe of Australian aborigines, and little or nothing will happen. Take it away from residents of California, and millions will die.

Edward O. Wilson, *Consilience*

The human population: 1930, 2 billion; 1961, 3 billion, 2008, 6.5 billion.

from Jan Zalasiewicz, *The Earth After Us*

INTRODUCTION

The first decade of the twenty-first century has been the strangest in my life, so far. Its defining moment was the destruction of the World Trade Center on 11 September 2001 which led directly to the invasion of Afghanistan and a barely disguised neo-colonial war against Taliban guerillas which has gone on ever since, and which will only end when America and her NATO allies tire of fighting.

9/11 was the beginning of George W. Bush and Tony Blair's much trumpeted "war on terror" which they claimed was world-wide and open-ended. It was a 'war' which gave Bush the specious casus belli for the invasion of Iraq in 2003 with all its disastrous consequences, an invasion which the neo-conservatives had been plotting since the late 1990s. It was not lost on observers that war, and a good deal of the terror that scarred the decade, were not only a direct result of America's aggressive policies in the larger Middle East, but were actually inflicted by US forces and their allies on the civilian populations of Afghanistan and Iraq.

The débâcle in Iraq is closely linked to the politics of oil. Nobody knows for sure when peak oil will occur, but it will be sometime this century and probably sooner rather than later. America's original plan, now abandoned, for the long-term occupation of Iraq was intimately bound up with this. The invasion was never about overthrowing a tyrant or bringing 'freedom and democracy' to the Iraqi people. If this were the case, America might just as well have invaded Darfur. Darfur, though, has no oil, while Iraq has the second largest known reserves in the world.

The global oil-based economy, however, is a major source of carbon emissions which in turn contribute to the current phase of global warming. Few scientists now doubt that this is occurring and that it is largely the result of human energy consumption in an overcrowded world. Climate scientists have consistently underestimated the speed of the process, however. As a result, the timescale for the melting of the Arctic and Antarctic ice sheets has had to be revised. It has been established, for example, that projections for ice loss in the Arctic for 2030, made only a few years ago, are already occurring. If these trends continue, the North Pole will be ice free in summer within a few years.

At the same time, human exploitation of the world's resources is having a cascade effect across the globe, creating a positive feedback loop which is destroying the Earth's flora and fauna. Deforestation, pollution, desertification, industrial scale agriculture, over-fishing, (and climate change), have cumulatively set in motion a mass extinction of species which biologists estimate will exterminate between 35 and 65 per cent of all plants and animals now living if allowed to proceed unchecked. The upper figure would place the current event in the same league as the great mass extinction at the Cretaceous-Tertiary boundary which sealed the fate of the dinosaurs.

These crises are deeply political in that only co-operative action on a global scale has any chance of heading them off. In the end, the mass extinction of species may turn out to be the most disastrous for humanity, though outside the fields of biology and ecology there is as yet little awareness of this.

Politics is part of the problem. It is narrow in focus, short-termist, and entrenched in notions of national self-interest. Politics as we know it is almost certainly a function of how humans evolved 200,000 years ago and because of this it will be very difficult to restructure. Understanding the evolutionary restraints on the human capacity for global collective action is a necessary first step.

An important aspect of our evolved nature is religion, which it is reasonable to assume is instinctive in humans. This does not make religious belief true. Indeed, if anything, religion is a stumbling block in our path when seeking a solution to global problems. For this reason, the resurgence of religion in the late twentieth and early twenty-first centuries cannot be ignored. Nor can its confrontation with science and reason which threatens to propel us into a new kind of Dark Age in which an increasingly sophisticated technology becomes the superstructure for a culture based on irrationality and superstition.

I have given this collection of essays the title *Fire Drill* because, although the crises of the decade 2001-10 are serious enough, when looked back on from a mid-century perspective, they are likely to be seen as a dry run, or drill, for what followed. The great question now is whether we can learn from what is happening and reverse 200,000 years of evolved human behaviour in order to avert far greater crises later this century.

As well as attempting an analysis of what has occurred in the past decade, *Fire Drill* is also a kind of personal record. In our daily existence there is often a disjunction between the visceral, contingent aspects of our lives and the greater patterns of human and natural history in which most of us have only insignificant roles, and of which we are only intermittently aware. The two cannot help but interact, however, if we think at all about what is going on in the wider world. So an essay on bird watching along the sands of Ynys Las, between Borth and the Dyfi estuary, leads to thoughts on the now global pollution of the Earth's beaches by our cast-off plastic artefacts which are ground down by the waves to become part of the sand itself.

Another essay starts from observation of the remains of the drowned forest which can be seen at Borth and Ynys Las and elsewhere along the mid Ceredigion coast, which leads to reflections on Cantre'r Gwaelod, the lost world of villages and towns which in legend is said to exist beneath the waters of Cardigan Bay. Nothing is static. Where will the line between sea and land be drawn in Ceredigion in a hundred years time? If global warming produces only a moderate rise in sea levels this century, Borth may well join the villages of Cantre'r Gwaelod, while Machynlleth, now far inland, may become a seaboard town.

We are in the process of changes that are so far-reaching that human existence can never be the same again; human nature itself may be undergoing one of the four or five great evolutionary and cultural transformations that the species has experienced in its history. Part of us embraces change, especially technological change, but part of us fears a profounder change that is not necessarily in our control. We try to avert our gaze and hope that it won't happen, even as we fear that it will. We busy ourselves with our lives, yet are haunted by our doubts.

11 SEPTEMBER, 2001

I was working in the office of *Planet* magazine when someone from the adjoining office put his head round the door and said, "Come and see this." And there on a plasma screen was the first Tower with smoke and flame engulfing its upper storeys. As we watched, a passenger plane swung behind the burning building and slammed into the second Tower. American voices off-camera moaned "Oh no!" and "Oh my God!" The camera held on the Twin Towers as they flamed furiously. An inset at the top of the screen showed the second plane swinging by and crashing, again and again, as if to emphasise the mesmeric quality of what we were seeing.

Later at home I watched the first Tower and then the second collapse vertically, as if they had been felled by demolition experts. There were shots at street level of people running, pursued by dense billowing smoke like the pyroclastic flow of a volcano. Later again I heard the mobile phone call from one of the doomed planes; a woman's tearful words to her husband, "I love you!" There were the agonised responses of onlookers interviewed to camera: "Why are they doing this to us, we are *good* people!"

It was impossible not to feel that you were watching a horrific event that would have equally horrific consequences. In retrospect, as the decade advanced, it became clear we had witnessed a defining moment in world history, and that the destruction of the Twin Towers by Al-Qaida might well be as consequential for humanity in the twenty-first century as World War I had been in the twentieth.

What those consequences would be was not immediately clear in 2001, except that under a neo-conservative president like George W. Bush, and given the shocked, angry reaction of the American people, they were likely to be bloody and vengeful. How bloody, and how vengeful, were beyond my imagination at the end of 2001, but when the Taliban refused to hand over Osama bin Laden it was clear that Afghanistan was in for a harsh reckoning. So we watched as America prepared its forces, and as B-52 bombers shattered the Taliban lines with "daisy cutters" and other high technology bombs and missiles. The Taliban were no match. An unknown number died in the bombardment; the rest fled into the mountains and disappeared in the semi-autonomous tribal borderlands in Pakistan. Bin Laden, the ostensible casus belli, disappeared too and has never been seen by Western eyes since. The victory seemed complete. America rewarded her allies in the Northern Alliance, including brutal psychopaths like Abdul Rashid Dostum, set up a puppet government under Hamid Karzai, left a ground force to search for bin Laden in the mountains, and went home.

For a while I thought that was the end of it. Some 3000 civilians had died in the attack on the Twin Towers; far more Afghan civilians had died in the invasion of Afghanistan, in the tradition of colonial reprisals of the past. Bin Laden had eluded capture, it was true, but revenge had been exacted on his harbourers and allies, and the infrastructure of Al-Qaida in Afghanistan had been destroyed.

What I had not reckoned with was that George Bush and his inner circle would use the destruction of the Twin Towers as an excuse to pursue a new aggressive policy in the Middle East. I did not know then that since the late 1990s neo-conservatives close to the President such as Dick Cheney, Donald Rumsfeld and Paul Wolfowitz, had been advocating the overthrow of Saddam Hussein and were only waiting for a plausible pretext.

An attack on American territory by Al-Qaida was hardly such a pretext, given that the secularist Saddam Hussein was an implacable enemy of the Islamist Osama bin Laden. That did not stop President Bush claiming that Saddam had given succour to Al-Qaida, even though no evidence for this was ever produced. In fact, in the months leading up to the declaration of war on Iraq, "evidence" amounted to no more than scare tactics, cynically manipulated to gather support at home and abroad for the invasion of a sovereign nation whose government the Bush administration had decided to destroy. Among these was a succession of Orange Alerts in New York prompted, it was claimed, by the threat of an "imminent" terrorist attack. (Once the war was under way, the Orange Alerts ceased.)

As the months passed and the American build-up of troops and ordnance gathered pace, claims of Iraqi support for Al-Qaida segued into claims about weapons of mass destruction. Despite years of UN sanctions and inspections, Saddam, it was alleged, had large stockpiles of chemical and biological weapons as well as the means to deploy them within forty-five minutes. He was still pursuing a nuclear capability and would achieve it within a few years. Colin Powell, in his presentation to the United Nations, showed blurry satellite images of vans that "might be" mobile chemical weapons units, buildings that were "believed to be" used to produce biological and chemical weapons. Not one of these allegations was true, and UN weapons inspectors like Hans Blix and Scott Ritter knew this to be the case. In an informative little book, *War on Iraq: What Team Bush Doesn't Want You to Know*, published in 2002, former UNSCOM inspector in Iraq, Scott Ritter, made a compelling case as to why Saddam's programme of weapons of mass destruction had been effectively deactivated by the weapons inspectorate. Judging by his shamefaced performance at the United Nations, Colin Powell, an essentially honest man, knew this too. So must Bush, Cheney, Rumsfeld and Condoleezza Rice, Bush's pliant National Security Adviser, have known. Unlike Powell, they brazened out their disinformation and lies with the appearance of utter conviction.

When, after the invasion, no weapons of mass destruction were found, the casus belli shifted retrospectively to "regime change". Saddam Hussein was an evil tyrant; the invasion had been undertaken to free the Iraqi people and as a warning to the other members of President Bush's "Axis of Evil".

No mention was ever made by the Bush administration of the fact that Iraq has the world's second largest proven oil reserve.

Indeed the question of oil as a motive for the invasion was effectively obfuscated by the flurry of pseudo-motives, and no
documentary evidence has ever been uncovered, to my knowledge, which points unequivocally to oil as the real motive for the
invasion. There is plenty of circumstantial evidence, however: the
fact that, after Baghdad fell, the Ministry of Oil was one of only
two ministries to be defended by American troops against the
widespread looting that was otherwise allowed to take place; the
fact that the embassy in the Green Zone is the largest US embassy
in the world; the fact that Bush and almost all his key advisers
have close links to the US oil industry and that lucrative contracts
in post-invasion Iraq were handed out to companies involved in
that industry; the fact that four giant military bases were built at
strategic points in Iraq, bases that are so large they have their own
bus services and are the size of moderate towns. These bases were
little discussed, but they were built for the duration. The long-
term plan in 2003 seems to have been for a permanent military
presence in Iraq which could be used to subdue Iran and Syria,
act as a shield to Israel, and control the flow of Iraqi oil. Oil
production in the US has already peaked; Venezuela, a major
producer on America's doorstep, has a government that is hostile
to it (though "regime change" there in form of a CIA-instigated
coup is a distinct possibility); China and India are becoming
major oil importers as they industrialise at a phenomenal pace;
America's current main overseas suppliers in West Africa are at
best unstable; it will take time to exploit the Alberta tar sands in
Canada that contain large deposits of oil which until recently had
been considered uneconomical. In a world with a dwindling
supply of oil and increasing demand, control of the Iraqi oilfields
is no small matter. This remains true, despite the temporary fall in
worldwide demand for oil following the financial crash and recession at the end of the decade.

From the day the Twin Towers were destroyed, George Bush
was assured of one ally in the form of Britain's Prime Minister,
Tony Blair. Under Blair, Britain would back America in whatever
course of action it decided to take. So Britain supported the
bombing of Afghanistan, and when Bush revealed his plan to
invade Iraq, Blair weighed in enthusiastically.

Tony Blair had one problem, however, which George Bush did not have. In Britain, the coming invasion was deeply unpopular. An estimated million people marched in protest against it in London and there were protest marches in many other cities and towns. When Blair staged a televised debate with ordinary people, the anger in the studio was palpable. But Blair had committed himself to the invasion and popular opposition was not going to deflect him. The protests were ignored. More troublesome was Andrew Gilligan's report on the *Today* programme, two months after the invasion had begun, which claimed that the Government-commissioned dossier on weapons of mass destruction had been knowingly exaggerated in order to justify the war. Alastair Campbell, Tony Blair's Director of Communications, immediately went on the attack, denying the allegation and threatening the BBC. It was all sound and fury, but the viciousness of Campbell's onslaught caused the BBC to lose its nerve. Greg Dyke, the Corporation's Director General, was forced to resign and Gilligan lost his job. The name of Gilligan's source, the Government chemical weapons expert, David Kelly, whom Gilligan had refused to expose, was leaked to the media and shortly afterwards David Kelly killed himself.

It was in 2002, during this build-up to the invasion, that I became intensely interested in politics. No one could doubt that Saddam Hussein was a brutal dictator, but in the 1980s he had been a favoured ally of America in the Middle East, despite the fact that he was known to have used chemical weapons against the Kurds. In the world of American realpolitik, Saddam was too useful then as a secular buffer against the militant Islamist state of Iran. Donald Rumsfeld had no problem shaking his hand in the '80s. After his rash invasion of Kuwait, however, and the First Gulf War, Saddam came to be seen as a liability. The time had come to destroy him.

Increasingly I had a sense of what it must have been like in 1937 or '38, knowing that Europe was building up to a catastrophic war and that all you could do was stand on the sidelines and watch. In 2002 and 2003, the most powerful state in the world was run by a cabal of men – Bush, Cheney, Rumsfeld, Wolfowitz – whose cynicism, brutality, and willingness to lie knew no limits.

At the height of the Vietnam War I had been living in Copenhagen. There I met a number of young Americans who had fled the USA to avoid the draft out of conviction that the war was immoral. I followed the progress of that war in the papers and on television, but it always seemed remote to me, perhaps because the British government had refused to take part in it. There was plenty of opposition to it in Denmark, though, especially in Copenhagen among young left-wingers and Marxist ideologues. Demonstrations, running street battles with the police, burning vehicles, barricades, were for a time common. Having witnessed the beginning of the 1968 student revolution at Birmingham University, and the intolerant and often underhand tactics of its leaders, I was suspicious of what was going on in Copenhagen. It was a suspicion that was strengthened by my dealings with the Marxist student bloc on committees at Copenhagen University. And so I stood apart from the Vietnam War, neither approving of it nor feeling obliged to oppose it.

I now think that was a wrong decision and that my distrust of the Marxists had led me into a false quietism. It took the invasion of Iraq a quarter of a century later to make me understand this. For it was impossible in 2003 to stand by and watch George W. Bush take the world into a war based on lies and for motives which were never openly declared. It was impossible not to feel involved, especially as Wales and Welsh regiments were complicit in Bush and Blair's irresponsible militarism. The Iraq War, I began to see, fitted a pattern of American aggression in recent decades and the war in Vietnam had been its template. Even though Britain had kept out of it, I should have been more responsive to what was going on in the early 70s.

When Iraq fell, George Bush had swaggered on the deck of an aircraft carrier, declaring major hostilities at an end, but it had been clear that the real war was about to begin, a war for which the American and British governments and military had failed to prepare. In the guerilla conflict that followed, several thousand American and allied soldiers were killed and many more badly wounded. A far greater number of Iraqi civilians were also killed, though the exact figure may never be known. From the beginning, the Americans refused to count civilian dead, muddying the

water by passing off innocent Iraqis killed by US troops as terrorists and insurgents. As a result of the occupation, though, and the
ensuing Sunni-Shia civil war, it is estimated that the figure may
run into hundreds of thousands.

As the war dragged on, atrocities by US and allied troops
began to be reported. Then came the exposure of Abu Ghraib
and the unforgettable photographs taken by American jailers
there for their own amusement – the hooded, naked prisoners;
prisoners forced to pile themselves naked on top of each other;
Lynndie England holding a naked man on a dog lead. All armies
abuse their enemies, but the best of them try to contain such
abuse. In the case of the American army in Iraq, it is clear that the
abuse and torture of Iraqi prisoners were tacitly sanctioned at the
highest level. It was a part of its hubris that the government of
George Bush believed it was above international law, even the
Geneva Conventions which America had signed. The existence of
the prison camp at Guantánamo with inmates imprisoned there
for years without being accused and without standing trial, has
been a daily reminder of this.

As the extent of what the Americans were doing in Iraq came
to light, I found myself rethinking my attitude to the United
States. George Bush never tired of talking at press conferences
about freedom and democracy. Freedom and democracy were
what they were fighting for in Iraq – in a late recension of the
justification for the invasion. As one frustrated GI was filmed
shouting to an angry mob of Iraqis as he faced them across rolls
of barbed wire: "We're here to bring you FUCKIN' FREEE-
DOM!" But what America and Britain in fact did was to bring
these ideals into disrepute.

From the start of the real war – the war of the Iraqi insurgents
against the occupiers – I was surprised how ill-disciplined the
American troops appeared to be; how easily they killed and
wounded bystanders in raids, or shot up the occupants of cars at
the slightest suspicion, or for no good reason at all. Given the
existence of car bombers, the nervousness of soldiers at check-
points or in convoys was understandable, but there were too many
incidents in which ordinary Iraqis including women and children
were killed in this way.

When the abuse and torture of suspects at Abu Ghraib Prison came to light, we were presented with an even grimmer image of how American soldiers operated. The White House and the Pentagon tried to pass this off as the work of a few bad apples in the lower ranks. It was clear, however, from the cynical comments of Donald Rumsfeld, the Secretary of Defense, that brutality of this kind had tacit approval at the top of the chain of command. Lynndie England and her kind may not have been obeying orders exactly, but they weren't disobeying any either.

I began to realise that what appeared at the outset to be a lack of discipline was in fact a pattern of accepted behaviour, a pattern that had first emerged in the Vietnam War. There too abuse and atrocities by American soldiers were widespread. There too when an incident was exposed in the media, as in the case of the massacre at My Lai, other ranks and junior officers shouldered the blame.

It might be objected that this is how armies of occupation behave and there is an element of truth in this. One can think of the Soviet army in Germany at the end of the Second World War. But it is not invariably the case. It was not by and large how the Allied armies behaved in Italy and Germany at the end of that war. It is certainly not what you expect from the army of a country which professes the highest ideals of freedom and democracy and which claims as its mission the promotion of these ideals throughout the world.

To an extent, of course, the cry of "freedom and democracy" can be dismissed as a cynical and scarcely credible veil for American global ambition. It is not the whole story, however, because very many Americans have internalised the image of themselves as the defenders of freedom and genuinely believe it. "We are good people!" the woman had cried as the Twin Towers came crashing down. It's possible to sympathise with her disbelief at what was happening, as it is with the frustrated soldier shouting about "fuckin' freedom" to the angry Iraqi crowd. In both cases, ordinary people were being confronted with a disquieting truth – that their self-image was at odds with what America actually does and with how it is perceived in many parts of the world. In such circumstances anger and frustration can easily turn to violence against those you believe you are trying to help. This is especially so if, as in Vietnam and Iraq, soldiers are faced with a people very different from themselves, whose culture it is tempting to see as inferior. Iraqis quickly become "towelheads" who, if they couldn't see that the occupation was for their own good, could be punished, and punished harshly in inverse proportion to the squandered ideals of the occupier.

Idealism then becomes a deeply complicating factor in America's relations with the rest of the world. For if you predicate your behaviour on belief in the self-evident rightness of your cause, it is easy to accept that any action you take, including the resort to violence, is – equally self-evidently – justified.

This assumption has come to be accepted as axiomatic in American popular culture. In an early television detective series like *Colombo*, the shambolic protagonist was a kind of down-at-heel Sherlock Holmes, solving crime through deductive logic. The starting point may have been a murder, but the interest lay in how Colombo was going to assemble the facts of the case, outwit the killer and make an arrest. There was very little overt violence on-screen, and Colombo never resorted to violence himself. Gradually, however, detective series became more overtly violent, and so did the detective-protagonist. It began to appear that there were two kinds of violence, that committed by bad people and that committed by the protagonist. In this manichean world, it is all right for the hero to beat up a suspect, even submitting him to what amounts to torture, because the end justifies the means.

When this fictional scenario is transferred to the real world, however, it cannot be sustained, because it takes no account of the way in which casual violence brutalises the perpetrator and corrupts the ideals in the name of which he or she acts. It takes no account, either, of how such violence is perceived by outsiders, especially when, as in Iraq, a whole nation is on the receiving end of it. Good men committing evil deeds from well-intentioned motives, is the root-stock of tragedy.

Even George Bush's claim to be promoting freedom and democracy in the world should be seen in this light, at least partially. There can be no doubt that the invasion of Iraq was opportunistic; that it had very little to do with freeing the Iraqi people and a lot to do with American hegemony in the Middle East and oil. Yet the hold on the American psyche of the idea of the nation's goodness is such that the most self-interested of actions can be promoted, to an extent quite genuinely, as a disinterested example of that goodness at work. Bush's claims may thus be cynical and sincere at the same time in a kind of irreconcilable schizophrenia, the end result of which is a tragedy on the Shakespearian model in which hundreds of thousands must die.

The damage of the past several years to America's standing abroad has been incalculable. The white noise of violence and lies has blotted out the country's great tradition of literature, art, music and science; has made invisible and seemingly insignificant the genuinely liberal voices who are as appalled as anyone at what has been done in their name. How America will recover, and whether it can recover, are questions that cannot be answered for now. It will take more than the shift to the Democratic presidency of Barack Obama, however; for the irreconcilable contradictions that are part of the deep structure of American culture are likely to remain.

THE WAR ON TERROR

Terror is an abstraction and as several commentators have pointed out, you cannot have a war against an abstraction. You can wage war against terrorist organisations who are fighting for control of a specific territory, such as the English war against the IRA in Northern Ireland, or the Spanish war against ETA in Euskadi; but you can only wage war on terror in a metaphorical sense.

George Bush's declaration of war on terror in 2001 was to some extent an expression of exasperation, because when he made it he did not know who the enemy was. It was a politician's rallying cry which successfully gathered the American people behind him, as well as much of the rest of the world, during the crucial first months after the assault on the World Trade Center.

When Al-Qaida claimed responsibility, though, America *did* have an enemy, with a geographical locus in Afghanistan and with a known leader, Osama bin Laden. In 2001-02 it seemed that the Bush administration was going to pursue a conventional war of revenge against bin Laden and, when they refused to hand him over, against his Taliban protectors. Leaving aside what motivated the attack on New York in the first place, the American response seemed understandable to many observers.

There were two problems, however. One was that Al-Qaida was fissiparous and its cells could be anywhere in the world, making it more difficult to attack than it first seemed. The other was that Bush's metaphoric war was not on terror of any kind, but on Islamist terror. The administration tried to obscure this in propaganda linking the American situation with the struggle of governments like that of Sri Lanka against Tamil separatists and other geographically limited terrorist movements. This was never pursued with any vigour, though. There was to be no world-wide "war on terror" led by the Americans, partly because terrorist organisations as diverse as Al-Qaida and the Tamil Tigers could not be defeated in the same way, but mostly because, from the beginning, the Bush administration was concerned only with terror that affected American interests.

Things began to go awry when the war on terror, meaning the war on militant Islam, became linked in American and British propaganda with the promotion of freedom and democracy – yet more abstractions, presented this time as universal values. Universalism is a slippery concept, however, and gives cause for suspicion when it is invoked on behalf of a political and economic system which you just happen to espouse. Its teleology – in this case that democracy is the best possible form of government to which all peoples aspire, and that America and Britain are themselves models of democracy – is a familiar one. The promoter of universal values is at their apex, a position from which wars of aggression can be launched on the grounds that they are fought to protect those values, or to bring them to people less fortunate or less advanced than themselves.

When, after destroying Al-Qaida's bases in Afghanistan, and ousting the Taliban, the Bush administration turned its attention on Iraq, "freedom and democracy" became one of its battle cries. The Coalition of the Willing was gathered under its banner, and when France opposed the invasion in the Security Council, it was disparaged in a diplomatic row in public that was unprecedented among Western nations since the Second World War. The French were vilified as cheese-eating surrender-monkeys, and French fries became Freedom fries for a while. The spat was conducted by the Americans at kindergarten level. Freedom, it seemed, meant freedom to follow the Bush administration into whatever war it chose to conduct.

Far from bringing freedom and democracy to Iraq and Afghanistan, however, the American interventions brought misery and destruction. Hardly any of the Bush administration's stated aims were achieved. The Taliban were not defeated, they melted into the mountains and are once again on the offensive in a war that is likely to end only when America and NATO withdraw from Afghanistan. For what began as a war against a hardline regime that was feared and hated by many Afghans, has segued into a patriotic war fought against an external aggressor. Moreover, opium production, which the allies want to eliminate and which had been severely curtailed under the Taliban, is now encouraged by the insurgents who use it to fund their operations. Osama bin Laden, too, has eluded capture, periodically taunting America and her allies in videotaped messages.

Things are only a little better in Iraq, despite the much-touted "Surge" and the turning of Sunnis against Al-Qaida as a result of the movement's brutality and fanaticism. The number of daily bombings and shootings has fallen dramatically, but Baghdad is still one of the most dangerous cities on Earth, its ethnically cleansed districts separated from each other by concrete barriers. Few Westerners dare venture beyond the Green Zone, even now, without a military escort.

What will happen once the Americans pull out, as Barak Obama has promised, is uncertain. Muqtadr al Sadr has only stood down his militia, the Mehdi Army. He, and it, are still to be reckoned with in the power struggle that is likely to take place. The bitter enmity between the Sunni and Shia has also to be resolved, as well as the problem of the displaced, and in many cases dispossessed, internal and overseas refugees. It is by no means certain that the current democratic structure will survive; government is weak and riven by factions; corruption is widespread; the loyalty of the newly established police and armed forces is an unknown quantity; so too is the role of Iran, Syria and Saudi Arabia, when the occupation ends. There is much unfinished business in Iraq.

It is the first great political irony of the twenty-first century that the war on terror has increased Islamic terrorism in ways that were entirely predictable but which Bush and his advisers, and Tony Blair with them, did not want to contemplate. After the invasion of 2003, Iraq, which had been free from Al-Qaida under Saddam Hussein, became a fertile recruiting and training ground for terrorists and a focus for Al-Qaida's activities. A consequence of the invasion of Afghanistan is that terrorist violence has also spread to Pakistan, and not just in the semi-autonomous tribal regions in the North, threatening to undermine the pro-Western government in Islamabad.

Moreover, the appalling death-toll among civilians in Iraq and Afghanistan, coupled with revelations of systematic torture and abuse of prisoners at Abu Ghraib, Bagram, and Guantánamo, and America's continued support for Israel in its determination to undermine any chance of a viable Palestinian state, have politicised a generation of young Muslims in Britain, who see the events of the current decade as an open assault on Islam by America and her allies. The London bombings of 7 July 2005 were a direct result of this perception, as evidenced in the martyrs' videos left behind by two of the bombers, Shehzad Tanweer and Mohammad Sidique Khan. The connection was vehemently denied by Tony Blair at the time, but it is beyond doubt. Blair's denial was another in the series of lies we have been told since 11 September 2001. Britain and America are in greater danger today from terrorist attacks by Islamic militants than ever before.

There is a further irony – and one we will pay a heavy price for – in that the more Bush and Blair claimed to be promoting freedom and democracy abroad, the more they undermined them in their own countries. The Patriot Act in the United States and a series of quickly cobbled together Acts of Parliament in Britain, have eroded civil liberties and the rule of law, substituting for them greater arbitrary power for the police, the secret services and the government. We were assured that such measures were taken for our own good, "good" here meaning safety. By a sleight of hand, "safety" was understood to mean "freedom", which by extension was also understood to include "democracy". The government was doing its best for us, we were told, based on information which, for the most part, had to be kept secret. It was a question of trust. Under the new laws, those who are innocent have nothing to fear.

The trouble is, Tony Blair forfeited that trust by lying so blatantly in the build-up to the invasion of Iraq and during its aftermath. I am not suggesting there was a conspiracy by New

Labour to undermine civil liberties – many of the new laws and restrictions were probably panic measures pushed through by a government out of its depth and unwilling to face the consequences of its actions; but its Thatcherite mentality made the accretion of power to government and the police seem natural and at one level even trivial, the only important freedom being the freedom to consume.

The new anti-terror laws have nonetheless been used against anti-war protesters and even, notoriously, against an aged heckler at a Labour Party conference. Had they been in force in the 1960s and 70s under a government like Tony Blair's they would undoubtedly have been used against the Welsh language movement, and may well be so used in the future if non-violent direct action returns to Wales. New Labour has been authoritarian and centralist despite its Thatcherite propaganda about empowering the people by extending their right to choose. For "choice" here does not mean devolving power to local government, it means creating an atomised society in which rail passengers become "customers" and students enter into a business agreement with universities that includes a degree as part of the deal. Thirty years of Thatcherism have depoliticised society, making it more difficult to mobilise people against the steady erosion of civil and legal rights that are fundamental to a democratic state.

Politicians rarely examine their motives in public and rarely admit mistakes. On the contrary, they are adept at covering their tracks with lies, and through public enquiries, chaired by establishment figures, who turn in verdicts favourable to the government which appointed them. It is not surprising therefore that neither George W. Bush nor Tony Blair has ever given the slightest hint that the invasion of Iraq was a huge political blunder. Nor have they expressed genuine regret, let alone remorse, for the hundreds of thousands of deaths that are a direct result of their policies. All things being equal, Bush and Blair should be tried for war crimes at The Hague, though this is never going to happen.

Failure to acknowledge the profound errors of judgement in the invasion of Iraq and the handling of the occupation is a serious problem; it means that political leaders are unwilling to consider the causes of Islamic terrorism on anything other than their own self-serving terms, according to which America and Britain are forces for good, while the terrorists are hate-filled and evil. America, especially, appears to believe it has done nothing to deserve the attacks on its embassies and its military personnel across the Muslim world, or, after 11 September 2001, on its home territory. This is not how the situation is perceived in many Muslim communities.

The way to defuse the terror attacks is to acknowledge that under British and French, and then American hegemony, the West has pursued a ruthlessly self-interested policy in the Middle East, from the Anglo-French division of territory after World War I, to the establishment of the state of Israel at the expense of the Palestinian Arabs, through the overthrow of Mohamed Mossadeq, the democratically elected prime minister of Iran, to support for the house of Saud and, while it suited the Americans, of Saddam Hussein. At no point have freedom and democracy in the region been of interest to the Western powers. What has mattered has been securing and keeping dominance over it; and the overwhelming reason for this has been its vast reserves of oil.

Until Western politicians are willing to admit this, and until they are willing to address the injustices their own policies have helped to create, Islamic terrorism is unlikely to be contained. Indiscriminate bombing by the US Air Force, small or large-scale invasions, the overthrow of leaders unpopular in American and Israeli eyes by assassination and other means – in other words business as usual as far as Western policies toward the Middle East are concerned – will only serve to spread Islamic terrorism, both in the Middle East and among radicalised young Muslims in Britain and elsewhere in Europe. Shehzad Tanweer and Mohammad Sidique Khan's videoed statements should be taken seriously. The destruction of the Twin Towers and the bombings in London were a direct result of the deeply flawed policies of America and Britain in the Middle East over the past half century, not the least of these being American policy toward Israel. This has been so blatantly pro-Israeli at the expense of the Palestinians that it has created a divide in the region which will be extremely difficult to resolve. Yet it must be resolved and in a way that is unequivocally fair both to the Israelis and the Palestinians – which means creating an independent and viable Palestinian state while preserving the territorial integrity of Israel as it was before the 1967 war. At present only America could conceivably do this.

However, an honest admission by the United States that its policies in the Middle East have been disastrous for the region, together with an expressed determination to right wrongs that have spread suffering from generation to generation, are so unlikely to be forthcoming – even from Barack Obama's administration – that what I have suggested is in danger of seeming naïve. Powerful nations do not do such things. They use their power, economically, politically and diplomatically, to persuade or cajole less powerful nations to do what they want, and if this fails they use force. Powerful nations rarely act altruistically. International aid programmes may seem to suggest otherwise, but funds set aside for this in countries like Britain and America dwindle into insignificance when compared to the budget for the military. Powerful nations can afford such gestures; the real investment, however, is elsewhere.

This being so, it is likely that as we move deeper into the twenty-first century yet more atrocities will be committed by Islamic terrorists in Britain, as well as in America and against their allies and interests abroad. In turn, this will impel the drift toward "strong" government that we have seen since 11 September 2001 – both in terms of threats toward, and bombing raids on, countries like Iran and Syria, either by the Americans or their Israeli surrogate; and the further erosion of legal and civil liberties at home.

Freedom and democracy, much touted but poorly understood by Bush and Blair, have been compromised almost beyond belief in a short space of time and in pursuit of a chimera, war against an abstraction, the war on "terror".

TONY BLAIR

Tony Blair was the strangest Prime Minister to govern so far in my lifetime. When he led the Opposition and during his first years in office, he looked boyish; he had the nervous smile that jammed itself into a broad grin and the impulsive hand gestures of an ambitious but socially awkward sixth former. He never lost those features, even during the strain of the build-up to the invasion of Iraq, even in the final years of his third term when he was under intense pressure to go.

When he first came to prominence as the moderniser who restructured the Labour Party and made it electable in the post-Thatcher era, he seemed merely an able politician. He was, however, clearly a Thatcherite, and his "rebranding" of the party as New Labour barely disguised the fact that under his control it became a modern Conservative party, outplaying the Tories at the game they had invented. Those who voted for New Labour in the belief that they were voting for a socialist party (slightly revamped) were deluding themselves.

It was after 11 September 2001, however, that other aspects of Blair came into focus, turning him into one of the most fascinating of post-war prime ministers, and one of the most dangerous.

His immediate expression of sympathy for America after the destruction of the Twin Towers, and his offer of help, seemed natural enough. Similar sentiments were expressed by governments around the world. What was not immediately clear was the extent to which Blair was willing to stand "shoulder to shoulder" with Bush, and how far he would go to demonstrate that the "special relationship" between the two countries was alive and well. This became a serious issue when, after bombing the Taliban into apparent oblivion, Bush turned his gaze on Iraq with the clear intention of toppling Saddam Hussein.

It was at this point that the school prefect in Blair came into its own as he took on the role of intermediary between the Bush administration and recalcitrant nations like France which were refusing to support the coming invasion. Blair passed himself off as the man of moderation who had George Bush's ear; who persuaded the President to keep on trying for a UN mandate in order to give the invasion a semblance of legality. (This was something Blair needed himself, in fact, because it would make it easier to persuade Parliament, and perhaps the people, that the coming war was justified. It is most likely that Bush went through these diplomatic motions for this reason alone.)

To many, Blair's attempt at Henry Kissinger-style shuttle diplomacy seemed not so much the work of a mature politician as that of a sycophant, and as he scampered between Europe and America, the image of him as Bush's poodle – a gift to cartoonists – was born. It was a sobriquet he deserved because his intervention as an "honest broker" was either naïve or dishonest. Even from the sidelines, it was clear that the Bush administration was going to take America to war, with or without the sanction of the UN, with or without the backing of countries like France. Allies were nonetheless useful to give credence to the invasion, and a rag-tag "Coalition of the Willing" was got up, composed of countries who saw advantage in backing the superpower. But it was always America's war and was going to happen because the USA was powerful enough (or so the Bush administration believed in 2002) to assert its will anywhere in the world.

Blair's behaviour in 2002 and early 2003 became increasingly bizarre. He initiated a series of "debates" with ordinary people around the country, the aim of which was to persuade the populace that the war was justified. Television footage, however, showed him facing angry audiences who did not believe a word he said and who vigorously attacked his support for US policy.

Blair's reaction to this was noticeable. He repeated time and again that he "may be wrong" but that he was doing what he "honestly believed" to be right. He would say this with an anguished look on his face and with elaborate gestures of the hands. He made similar statements in the House of Commons and in press interviews; everything, it seemed, was being staked on his sincerity. It may be that he had got it all wrong on Iraq, but he was following his conscience and so he was justified. A twist on this was the appeal to history: history would judge whether he had made the right decision – with the implication that history would decide that he had. There is an irony here in that Blair, who was so keen to appeal to history (in its future manifestation), seemed so ignorant of the history of Iraq and Britain's role in it, as well as, more generally, the history of ill-considered overseas adventures of the kind America was committed to, with Britain as its satrap.

In taking this line Blair created a problem for himself, because the more he protested his sincerity, "hand on heart", the more insincere he appeared to be. It is unusual for a prime minister to appeal to the country in this way, reducing a major issue of war or peace to one of trust in the fact that, right or wrong, he was sincere, as if that settled the matter and we should all fall in line. Blair's religious belief – something which he was otherwise careful to keep out of the political arena – seems to have seeped through here. Suddenly he was not speaking the language of realpolitik but the language of the confessional, baring his anguish and his conviction before Parliament and the people instead of the priest.

The result was that it was impossible *not* to doubt him; the more so because week by week Blair's wholesale commitment to the invasion became ever more clear. It is possible that he started out in good faith; perhaps he was even sincere (though catastrophically wrong). His attempts to persuade us, however, led him into a maze of prevarications, evasions, and in the end lies, the most glaring of which was the "dodgy dossier" in which the grounds for invasion were doctored under government pressure.

Blair has never publicly acknowledged any of this; the appeal is still to the court of history, and of course the court has not yet sat. For the time being, he appears as a Dickensian hypocrite, so armoured in self-righteousness that it is impossible for anyone, other perhaps than his confessor, to know whether he is aware of the enormity of what he has done. For, in a mere six years, he brought Britain into disrepute through his support of an invasion that cost thousands of lives, displaced millions more, and destroyed the infrastructure of Iraq – all because of his apparent belief in the inviolability of our "special relationship" with the USA, even when that country was in the hands of a reckless and brutal regime.

During his appearance before the Chilcot Inquiry, Blair sidestepped the question of responsibility by arguing that very few Iraqi civilians were killed during the invasion itself. Most civilian deaths, he insisted, had occurred during the occupation and had been inflicted not by coalition forces but by Iraqi insurgents. This is at best disingenuous. Iraqi civilian casualties have been notoriously difficult to estimate because of the US refusal to count them, and because many Iraqis killed by coalition troops have been passed off as insurgents. A survey in *The Lancet*, however, which is perhaps as close as we will ever get to a real figure, estimated that US troops had killed between 132,000 and 246,000 civilians – 31 per cent of civilian deaths during the occupation. Even if Blair's assertion were true, the obvious retort is that ultimate responsibility lies with those who planned and executed the invasion since this created the conditions for what amounted to a civil war. Blair was given an easy ride at the Inquiry, however, and the retort was never made. When Gordon Brown appeared before Chilcot, he gave the same self-exculpating account. He too was not challenged.

Blair's sincerity card was closely related to that of humility, and once again his Christian faith seeped through into the public sphere. In deliberately seeking tête-à-tête sessions with members of the public during the build-up to the war, sessions which he and his advisers must have known would be hostile, Blair revealed a propensity for actions that he may have thought of as an *imitatio Christi*, but which came across as a very strange form of willed, pseudo-martyrdom. Those sessions must have been exhausting and not a little humiliating. They served no purpose other than to cast him in the light of the agonised soul.

Yet Blair's humility, like his sincerity, is open to question. In his last couple of years in office, he worried endlessly, and publicly, about his political "legacy", hoping now that it would be the

Northern Ireland agreement, now reforms at home. Never to my knowledge was it the invasion and continuing war in Iraq and the devastation and suffering that he had more than a hand in causing. Far from humility, this argues for a massive ego. It is not for the individual in the public arena to decide what his legacy will be; it is certainly not for the Christian to try to fix that legacy in advance. Only the future can decide that – the "court of history" which earlier he had been so keen to invoke. This attempt to establish his legacy before the dust has settled (something he shares with George Bush) is perhaps the one significant and unintended indication that he knows Iraq will be that legacy, and that it will not be a positive one. It is, in other words, the tiniest suggestion of his knowledge of his guilt, which he can never admit, any more than George Bush can. History may be the judge, but Blair is determined to be his own advocate before the court has even convened – he was not trained as a lawyer for nothing. We have still to hear, however, the case for the prosecution.

Tony Blair's career since he left Parliament is almost as interesting as his ten years in office and casts a significant light on his premiership. His conversion to Roman Catholicism was widely predicted, but freed from considerations of political expediency in a still secular Britain, he has given full rein to his religious convictions, foregrounding them in a very public way.

One of his first acts was to establish The Tony Blair Faith Foundation, the aim of which, according to its "mission statement", is to "promote respect and understanding about the world's major religions and show how faith is a powerful force for good in the modern world." The Foundation is not merely an inter-faith think tank, however. There is a practical, charitable side to its work, as the mission statement makes clear: "…the Foundation will use its profile and resources to encourage people of faith to work together more closely to tackle global poverty and conflict. By supporting such inter-faith initiatives, the Foundation will help underline the [sic] religion's relevance and positive contribution."

What this means in practice is spelled out in a press release posted on one of Blair's websites, The Office of Tony Blair: "Tony Blair launches campaign urging faith action to eliminate deaths from malaria". The campaign, called "Faith Acts Together", aims to eradicate the scourge of malaria, which kills a million people worldwide each year, by encouraging inter-faith participation in eradication and prophylactic projects. Many people coming together and contributing small amounts, the press release reminds us, can change the world: "…just one £5 or $10 insecticide-treated bed net can protect an entire household."

Another press release announced Blair's appointment in 2008 as Howland Distinguished Fellow at Yale University, which involved him in teaching on the "Faith and Globalisation Initiative", a three-year collaborative project between the Yale Divinity School, the University's School of Management and the Tony Blair Faith Foundation. The press release is a little short on detail: "The course will explore issues concerning the public roles of religious faiths in the context of globalisation. The potential for religious faith to bring the world's people together rather than drive them apart will be explored through the seminar and made available to a world audience through a <u>multi-media website</u>", is all it says.

The Initiative, with its characteristic blend of religion, business (and by implication, politics), reflects a key element in Blair's psychology and thinking which must have made his ten years as Prime Minister deeply frustrating on occasion. On 5 February 2009, he gave an address to the National Prayer Breakfast, in the presence of the newly installed President Barack Obama. The address is revealing in this context – at times unintentionally so.

Blair had his first "spiritual awakening", he told his fellow breakfasters, at the age of ten. His father had just suffered a serious stroke, and at school one of his teachers suggested that they kneel down and pray for his recovery. Blair Senior was a "militant atheist", however, and the boy felt he ought to tell his teacher. "'That doesn't matter,' my teacher replied, 'God believes in him. He loves him without demanding or needing love in return.'"

"That is what inspires," Tony Blair reflects: "the unconditional nature of God's love. A promise perpetually kept. A covenant never broken." "And in surrendering to God," he concludes, "we become instruments of that love."

Is that what Blair thought he was during his premiership, an instrument of God's love? The possibility is disturbing. He clearly sees a key role for religion in the management of human affairs. His Faith Foundation, he reminds his audience, aims to bring people of different faiths together in a spirit of harmony and good will. "But as someone of faith," he continues, "this is not enough. I believe restoring religious faith to its rightful place, as the guide to our world and its future, is itself of the essence. The twenty-first century will be poorer in spirit, meaner in ambition, less disciplined in conscience, if it is not under the guardianship of faith in God."

This is to put religion at the heart of politics, and mindful perhaps that his words would be scrutinised by the non-religious as well as the religious, he immediately adds a disclaimer: "I do not mean by this to blur the correct distinction between the realms of religious and political authority." He then proceeds with an anecdote which inadvertently reveals that this is precisely what he means. "In Britain," he elaborates, "we are especially mindful of this. I recall giving an address to the country at a time of crisis. I wanted to end my words with 'God bless the British people'. This caused complete consternation. Emergency meetings were convened. The system was aghast. Finally, as I sat trying to defend my words, a senior civil servant said, with utter disdain: 'Really, Prime Minister, this is not America you know.'"

At the National Prayer Breakfast, held in Washington DC, and attended by leading figures in American business, politics and religion, the anecdote no doubt raised the smile it was calculated to produce. Blair, however, fails to perceive that its import is the opposite of what he meant, for it reveals how close he was during his premiership to blurring the distinction between politics and religion which he began by saying was so important. Moreover, in telling the joke against the stuffy British Civil Service, he fails to see that the anonymous senior civil servant was right. In Britain, the separation of church and state is still fundamental to the functioning of politics, while in America that separation is constantly being broken down. There have been public protests against the National Prayer Breakfast itself on precisely these grounds.

Toward the end of his address, Tony Blair considers the nature of leadership. "Courage in leadership," he reflects, "is not simply about having the nerve to make difficult decisions or even in doing the right thing since oftentimes God alone knows what the right thing is." It is, he claims, adapting a term from Christian theology, "to be in our natural state – which is [not sin, apparently, but] one of nagging doubt, imperfect knowledge, and uncertain prediction – and to be prepared nonetheless to put on the mantle of responsibility and to stand in full view of the world, to step out when others step back, to assume the loneliness of the final decision-maker, not sure of success but unsure of it."

It is impossible not to take this as a veiled allusion to his role in the invasion of Iraq which made him a hero in the United States and deeply unpopular in Britain. The figure he projects here is that of the Leader – Roman in bearing; alone, even aloof, with the burden of ultimate responsibility; fearless when it comes to making unpopular decisions which he believes to be right. It is a long way from the British tradition of collective government by Cabinet, where the Prime Minister is first among equals.

No doubt, like George W. Bush, Tony Blair wishes fervently that he could put Iraq behind him, but it is the spectre at the feast of his very public religiosity. When he resigned as Prime Minister and announced that he was also resigning his seat at Sedgefield, he was interviewed by Chris Lloyd, Political Editor of *The Northern Echo*. There is an external link to the interview on The Office of Tony Blair website, so he or his team must think it shows him in a good light. It is certainly respectful and not very probing. Chris Lloyd asks the obvious questions: What are his immediate plans? What does the role of Middle East peace envoy entail? What did the Queen say when he went to Buckingham Palace? And so on.

But when the issue of Blair's political legacy is raised, and the ex-Prime Minister gives an answer which focuses entirely on domestic politics, even the polite Chris Lloyd feels impelled to mention Iraq. "Iraq will obviously be part of that legacy," he interjects. "How do you feel when the nightly news bulletins are full of stories of carnage?"

Blair must have expected Iraq to come up, but his answer is bizarre. "If we hadn't acted, it wouldn't be on the news," is his first response. This is glaringly true. If Bush and Blair had not invaded Iraq, the insurgency and the vicious civil war between Sunni and Shia would not have happened and there would be nothing for the media to report. As if realising that this is not quite the way to put it, Blair changes tack in an attempt to divert the question away from the consequences of the invasion: "They have uncovered the mass graves of several hundred thousand people murdered under Saddam Husein, and there were a million casualties in the Iran/Iraq war," he says; adding in explanation, "It wasn't that people weren't dying before, it was that it wasn't on our television screens." This is partly true, though Saddam's gas attack on the Kurds was widely reported, as was the general barbarity of his regime.

Blair is digging himself into a hole without, it seems, being entirely aware of it. For the implication of what he is saying is that the appalling loss of life during and after the invasion may well be comparable to the mass deaths under Saddam, it is just that we are more aware of the former because of increased media access to Iraq after 2003. Moreover, in mentioning the Iran-Iraq war, he inadvertently raises the issue of earlier Western interference in the region, when Saddam was seen by America as a useful ally against the revolutionary Islamic state of Iran. If there were a million casualties in that war, then by encouraging Saddam's attack on that country, America was complicit in their deaths.

"The most powerful thing," he continues, "is that the Iraqis who have been elected to their government will say yes, it is terrible that we have had the carnage of Saddam and now we have the carnage of the terrorists, why should we have to have one or the other?" Again this is no doubt true, but it obfuscates a deeper truth which is that the insurgency and civil war were entirely predictable consequences of the invasion and its botched aftermath, for which he, Tony Blair, as George Bush's staunchest ally, must bear a good deal of responsibility. Moreover, this account leaves out of the reckoning the carnage inflicted by allied troops, especially the Americans, during and after the invasion, which in turn fed into the insurgency against the occupiers.

The nearest he comes to answering the question is when he says: "I don't regret removing Saddam." Even here, though, as if anticipating further questions, he dismisses the consequences of that removal: "You can argue about all these issues like deba'athification of the army and disbanding it and so on." The hole gets deeper. You cannot "argue" about these issues as if, well, on the one hand…, on the other hand. By the time Blair said this, it was universally acknowledged that the decision by L. Paul Bremer, head of the Coalition Provisional Authority, to embark on a process of deba'athification and to disband the Iraqi army within a fortnight of taking office, was a catastrophic error of judgement. Four hundred thousand trained soldiers were cast onto the streets with no work and no prospects, and in a country awash with arms. Bremer's decision was a major contributing factor to the insurgency against the occupying forces which followed. If Blair cannot see this, it raises a serious question about his judgement and his understanding of what really happened in Iraq after 2003.

His next attempt to dig himself out is worthy of Basil Fawlty's comment about his wife Sybil: "Special subject, the bleeding obvious." "The real reason we have got a problem in Iraq," he observes, "is that the enemy we face is fighting us"; adding, "it is not because someone somewhere ticked the wrong box." Well, you have to expect your enemy to fight you. And someone, somewhere, ticking the wrong box? Who could that be, as if the tens of thousands of civilian casualties, that were a consequence of the invasion, might be due to an administrative error?

But of course, in Blair's world, there was no administrative error, and no burden of responsibility for the invasion and its disastrous aftermath. It is all down to the inconvenience of an enemy that insists on fighting.

Perhaps by association with what he has just said, Blair goes on to reflect: "The worst moments are always when I hear about the deaths of our armed forces." Then in a last twist, as if he suddenly remembers what the question was, he concludes: "That's not to say that I don't have a great sense of responsibility for the decision making, I do," adding somewhat mysteriously, "but I also don't believe that their evil can entertain our respect."

Blair did not mention Iraq in answer to the question about his political legacy, but when it is raised, he flounders, he cannot confront the consequences of his actions or take any responsibility for them. It is unlikely that we will ever know what he really thinks. Perhaps not even Cherie Blair or his confessor knows, for it may be that Blair's denial is so deep that he himself believes the confused, glossed-over version of events he stumbles through in this interview.

Not least among the ironies of Blair's career is the fact that shortly after his resignation from Parliament, he was appointed Middle East envoy for the Quartet – the UN, the USA, Russia and the EU; his mission, to work toward a solution of the Israeli-Palestinian conflict. Perhaps the appointment was made on the assumption that someone who had a large hand in destabilising the Middle East in the first decade of the twenty-first century might have some idea of how to fix it. The insights on offer in his interview with Chris Lloyd make this a doubtful proposition.

In an article on the ABC News website, Philip Victor quotes an anonymous senior UN official to the effect that: "There's a view in the UN that he's not making any progress and that from all the status he brings to the position, he doesn't seem to be achieving anything." Since no one else has been able to achieve anything in the past forty years, this is perhaps no surprise, though Victor suggests that one of the reasons for Blair's lack of progress is that he is too busy making a fortune, close to a £10 million fortune, in fact, in the sixteen months following his resignation as Prime Minister. According to Victor, who draws on a report in *The Times*, £5.8 million of this came from speaking engagements (at $250,000 a time), the rest from consultancies with JP Morgan Chase and Zurich Financial Services (£2 million and £500,000 respectively), his salary from Yale, and his Prime Ministerial pension.

There was of course a vigorous rebuttal of the UN official's criticism from Blair's office. His role as the Quartet's envoy "takes up the largest portion of his time," it was claimed. Moreover, "No official of the UN or any other Quartet member has ever raised any such concerns with us." Perhaps, however, this is because no one really takes the role of the Quartet's envoy to the Middle East that seriously. Only America can change Israel's self-aggrandising policy toward the Palestinian Arabs which is one of the keys to a peaceful settlement.

It is interesting, nonetheless, to speculate on why Tony Blair accepted the post. Could it be that, having played the righteous warrior, wielding the two-edged sword of Democracy and Freedom, and witnessing its destructive consequences, he saw in the role of Quartet envoy to the Middle East an opportunity to redeem himself? It is noteworthy that in his career since stepping down as Prime Minister, Blair has gone out of his way to emphasise his desire to bring people of different religious faiths together, to show how the religions of the world can be a powerful force for good. This is the obverse of the previous ten years in which his policies, following those of that militant Christian George W. Bush, helped create a deep rift between the West and Islam which it may take generations to bridge.

For a Christian, however, redemption is only achieved through contrition and a full and true accounting of his sins. There is no evidence yet that Tony Blair is ready for this.

TORTURE

I once visited the torture chamber in the City Hall in Nuremberg. It was a large room built below street level. It contained a rack with a wooden windlass and various hand-forged iron tongs and pincers. There was also the Iron Maiden of Nuremberg, a container shaped like a mummy case, with a painting of a woman on its lid. On the inside of the lid were long, sharp iron spikes situated so that when it was closed they would pierce the eyes, the breast, the intestines, the genitals of anyone who was forced to lie in its coffin-like interior.

To get to the chamber we were guided along a narrow corridor where the holding cells were. These were about four feet wide and six feet long; each had a wooden door with an iron grill. Prisoners were chained there day and night in total darkness. They would have heard the screams of the tortured as they waited their turn.

These could also be heard by the City Fathers, for in the centre of the torture chamber there was a stone-built vent leading to a roomy chamber above. They could put their ears to this and listen to the confessions of the tortured below. They never had to see the victims.

That was in the Renaissance, a long time ago.

Growing up in the 1950s, it never occurred to me that I might one day live in a country that condoned torture – while denying it officially, of course. That went on elsewhere but not in Britain. The police might beat someone up during an interrogation, but if they were caught they paid the penalty, because force amounting to torture was strictly against the law. At the time, I, like most people, had no idea that torture was commonly practised in the British colonies, for this was kept away from public scrutiny.

That changed under Thatcher in the 1980s when torture in the form of hooding, stress positions, beatings, was regularly practised by the British Army and the intelligence services in Northern Ireland. Even this, though, could be passed off as an anomaly which came to an end, or so it was claimed, when the practice was exposed in the media. In the 1980s and 90s it was still possible to feel that you lived in a civilised country where torture was considered by most people to be abhorrent, and where information obtained by it was inadmissible in British courts.

In the first decade of the twenty-first century, however, Britain became a torturing nation again. At one end of the scale this "merely" involved the inhumane treatment of suspects, some of whom were kept in solitary confinement in high security prisons like Belmarsh without prospect of a trial. A number of these detainees cracked under the strain and had to be transferred to psychiatric units. At the other end, British soldiers were directly involved in the torture of prisoners in Iraq, in some cases beating innocent men to death. The "bad apples" excuse was paraded at the trial of a few low-ranking soldiers whose activities were exposed in the press and could not be ignored. Rather than do the torturing ourselves, however, it has been simpler to collude with the Americans in their practice of "extraordinary rendition", whereby suspects are flown in unmarked planes to countries like Jordan that are only too keen to shoulder the torturer's burden. In other cases, suspects have simply been extradited to their country of origin. When organisations like Amnesty International have objected on the grounds that these individuals are likely to be tortured or killed, the British Government has responded that the Algerian or the Egyptian government has given guarantees that this will not be the case. Many of those compulsorily returned in this way are never seen again. British nationals detained in Iraq and Afghanistan and at Guantánamo have also reported that British Intelligence officers were present during their interrogation. In most cases they took no part in the ensuing torture though their presence involved them by association.

Guantánamo, Abu Ghraib, Bagram, names no one had heard of ten years ago, have become synonyms for inhumanity and torture, mostly to be sure on the part of the Americans but in many cases with the complicity of the British. Such prisons, and the unnamed ones around the world that we do not know about, were the grand torture chamber of the Anglo-American alliance where the promoters of the War on Terror, George W. Bush and Tony Blair, could leave the dismantling of humanity to others, never coming face to face with the wreckage. Like the City Fathers of Nuremberg in their fur-fringed robes, they lived above ground and could go home in the evening to their families with a clean conscience.

But torture is a deep stain which does not readily wash out, affecting not only Bush, Blair, and their ministers, but all of us who go about our business and refuse to hear the screams in dark places that are far away, but very near. Torture has been committed in our name and for our own good, as our leaders assured us, even though every human being who is strung up and broken diminishes us and diminishes our capacity to create a society and a state based on humanity and mutual respect.

There are of course pragmatic arguments for torture, exemplified by the "ticking bomb" hypothesis. If you know there is a bomb hidden in London or New York that may kill many thousands, and if you have in your hands an individual who you suspect knows where that bomb is, then isn't torture justified to force its whereabouts out of him for the greater good? It is possible to agree to the use of torture in such circumstances while deploring its use generally. The problem is that torture cannot be confined in this way; nor do proponents of the hypothesis intend it to be. It is a scare scenario designed to instil in the populace a fear of what might happen if torture were not used. If there are only hours to go before the bomb explodes, then we have to leave it to the government and the intelligence services to make a decision. They would not torture anyone needlessly, so the argument goes; there would have to be compelling reasons.

In *The Alan Partridge Show*, the comedian Steve Coogan in the character of Alan Partridge says in frustration in an argument with his Russian wife: "Well, the police would hardly have arrested them if they hadn't done something, would they!" And that is the trouble with the ticking bomb hypothesis. It asks us to take on trust the politicians, the secret services and the military when time and again they have shown themselves – especially the politicians – to be untrustworthy. Justifying torture on the basis of the ticking bomb segues into justifying torture generally, because, the argument is, you cannot be sure what these men might know, how many lives might be saved if they can be made to confess.

This begs the counter-argument that information gained under torture is notoriously unreliable. When pain becomes unendurable, most people will say anything to make it stop. What a tortured individual confesses may be the truth, or it may be what he thinks his torturers want to hear, or indeed it may be anything that comes into his head.

Pragmatic arguments are in any case overridden by the moral one. Torture is not something that can be contained. It cannot be used judiciously and with precision, the torturer going home after a day's work to play with his children, talk with his wife, relaxing over a glass of wine. Torture debases all these things, makes of them a shiny mask that conceals the inhumanity within. We recognise this in the workings of the Nazi regime in Germany. The horrors of the Gestapo, the SS, the medical experimenters like Dr Mengele, the death camps, turned the achievements of German culture to ashes, corrupting a nation for a generation.

Through their promotion of torture, the United States of America and Britain have stepped into this world. Well into the occupation of Iraq, there was an advert on British television for a make of car in which a dog is seen in the front passenger seat "laughing" and appearing to mime to a song – "I'm a man, yes I am…!" This scene is intercut with one showing a dog of the same breed, standing, leashed, its flanks quivering, while a human voice mimics its whimpers. The last frames show the "man"-dog accelerating away in the fast lane. Who would you rather be, the advert implies with a sneer.

I don't think that advert would have been made a decade ago. The second dog's abjectness and fear are ridiculed and dismissed. This isn't a world for losers, for the weak, for those who have been broken. Life sweeps on, triumphant and cruel, and unforgiving.

Behind it is the shadow of Guantánamo, Belmarsh, the unmarked planes, a society that, in the first decade of the twenty-first century, began to lose its hold on human decency.

THE BEGINNING OF SORROWS

During my lifetime there have been the following wars: the Second World War, the Korean War, the First and Second Vietnam Wars, the First and Second Iraq Wars, the Iran-Iraq War, the First and Second Chechen Wars, the First and Second Afghan Wars. There have also been smaller scale wars, colonial wars, and internecine wars, including war in Algeria, three wars between Israel and the Palestinians and the Arab states, war in Kenya, Malaya, East Timor, Nigeria, Sri Lanka, the former Yugoslavia; the list could go on.

Yet my generation in this corner of Northern Europe has been lucky. Conscription was abolished in Britain about eighteen months before I was due to be called up. No one in my generation has been forced into going to war. Earlier in the twentieth century it was different – an uncle of mine was wounded in South Africa during the Boer War, another in Mesopotamia during the First World War, and yet another had his health ruined by malaria contracted at Gallipoli. During the Second World War, a cousin was killed in Italy and another badly wounded in Holland. My father was in that war but didn't see action; he was injured in an accident loading ships in preparation for the Normandy landings. Compared to millions of others in the twentieth century, my family was lucky.

The pattern of wars varies. Some begin with jingoistic enthusiasm like the First World War only to become bogged down. When a war goes on for more than two or three years, and when casualties are high, it seems a rule that disillusionment sets in among soldiers and civilians. Only a short war can sustain the initial zeal of the public and the army. The Falklands War is an example. The expeditionary force left English ports to the sound of brass bands and Union Jack-waving relatives on the quaysides. We were going to see to the Argies. Yet the prime minister at the time, Margaret Thatcher, and her military planners were lucky. The British were better armed and trained but were fighting a long way from home with hazardous supply lines. They also met unexpectedly fierce resistance from the Argentinian Air Force. Had some of their exocet missiles not failed to detonate, had they sunk the fleet's aircraft carrier, the outcome of the war could have been very different. Chance more than anything meant that most people in Britain who remember the Falklands War think of it as a clean war, even a good war, of the kind that Tony Blair committed Britain to in Kosovo, and which he perhaps persuaded himself he was doing when he joined George W. Bush in the invasion of Iraq.

Other wars, however, are not entered into with enthusiasm. The Vietnam War overtook the American people by stealth. At first there were only US "advisers" in Vietnam; next there were support troops; then America was involved in a full-blown conflict with a death toll that rose and rose, and which the US military, despite its superior firepower, could not win. Fierce opposition by civilians in the United States, combined with the demoralisation of the army in the field, made the war impossible to conduct. It is the only war in my lifetime in which massive civil disobedience played a part – perhaps the major part – in forcing a Western government to end a war and concede defeat.

Other wars are opposed from the beginning. This was the case in Britain during the build-up to the Second Iraq War in 2002-03. Despite government propaganda, an estimated million people demonstrated in London against the invasion, and many hundreds of thousands in towns and cities elsewhere. The invasion had its supporters, including those who believed that an English government would not lie about an issue as important as the declaration of war. Generally, though, the mood was angry or subdued; even those who favoured war on the grounds laid out by Tony Blair had no real appetite for it. With the exception of initial support in the United States, the Second Iraq War and the Afghan War have been conducted by Western governments with limited enthusiasm among the people. The only reason there has not been more vigorous opposition since 2002-03 is that casualties have been light. Had British troops suffered a higher casualty rate, the government would have been forced by public opinion to end its part in the occupation. As it is, by 2007 even the government seemed to have lost its appetite for the war, withdrawing British troops from Basra and confining them to barracks at the airport.

My generation, I believe, has a rather skewed understanding of war. Because of the comparatively peaceful state of Western Europe in the past sixty years, we tend to see war as exceptional; an eruption of violence which temporarily breaches the norm, which is peace. The medievalist Geoffrey Shepherd used to say that in the Middle Ages peace was an interlude in war, and that war, or preparation for war, or recovery from war, was the norm. The same could be said for many parts of the world in the twenti-eth century. Britain was at war from 1899-1902, 1914-18, 1939-45, 1950-53, and 1982, leaving aside smaller colonial wars of independence in the 1950s and the war in Bosnia and Kosovo in the 1990s. That makes twenty-one years of war, twelve of them years of total war in which hundreds of thousands of soldiers and civilians were killed and the wealth of the nation squandered. The periods 1919-38 and 1946-56 were also dominated by these wars, either in recovery from devastation and exhaustion, or (in the late 1930s) in trying to avoid a renewal of war and, when that failed, rapidly re-arming for it. For fifty-five years out of a hundred, then, Britain was either at war, preparing for war, or suffering from its aftermath. From about 1950 to 1989, during the Cold War, Britain was also in a constant state of preparedness for nuclear war which involved a huge expenditure on intercontinental ballistic missiles, early warning systems, aircraft, and submarines.

The situation in the world is currently so volatile that it is impossible to predict five years ahead with any certainty. The twenty-first century, however, is likely to be just as dominated by war as was the twentieth. At the end of its first decade, Britain has already been at war for seven years, and not in self-defence but in wars of aggression in Iraq and Afghanistan; wars that have cost hundreds of thousands of civilian lives, have destroyed the infra-structure of these two countries, have created several million refugees, and may in retrospect be seen as having played a part in bankrupting America, the main aggressor.

Wars in the present century are likely to be resource wars for water, oil, essential minerals and metals, perhaps for agricultural land, too, as the Earth's limited resources come under pressure from overpopulation, and the understandable desire of the rest of the world to achieve a Western standard of living, even though this is unsustainable. These wars will probably be fought along the so-called North-South divide, with Western nations attempting to use superior military power to secure the resources they need. The First and Second Iraq Wars were the first of such wars, fought by the United States and her allies to secure hegemony over the oilfields of Kuwait, Saudi Arabia, and Iraq. That the second war did not turn out the way the Bush and Blair regimes planned is another matter.

The really large-scale wars, however, will most likely be fought between the already developed nations and nations like China whose rapid industrialisation makes it a serious threat. A war between Japan and China for hegemony on the Pacific Rim is possible. A war, perhaps a nuclear one, may yet be fought between India and Pakistan. There may also be wars that represent unfinished business, just as the Second World War can be seen as a continuation of the First. Those who hailed the end of the Cold War as a victory for American capitalism over Russian communism may have been too hasty. Russia lost its continent-wide empire almost overnight, but that does not mean that it saw 1989 as the end of its imperial ambitions or that it does not harbour a desire for revenge against its former client states, especially the Baltic nations, Poland and Ukraine. These nations were quick to apply for membership of NATO and the EU because they saw political and military integration with Western Europe as the best possible insurance against future Russian expansionism. That would not necessarily prevent a freshly armed and nationalistic Russian dictatorship from invading them, however, if it saw an opportunity. If Estonia, Latvia and Lithuania were overrun by a New Russia eager to expand its territory and wipe out the "shame" of 1989, what would the West do?

This raises an important question. War is always shattering

and rarely turns out as the aggressor intended. It involves incalculable human suffering and, under modern conditions, material destruction on a vast scale. This being so, what is it that makes humans, collectively, so willing to go to war? Instead of being the very last resort undertaken with regret, war is often seized on by politicians as the best means of achieving a desired foreign policy objective quickly. Diplomacy is then used as a kind of fog to disguise their true aims, and to engineer a casus belli.

It has been suggested that one reason why George W. Bush and Tony Blair were so insouciant about invading Iraq and Afghanistan is that they are ignorant of history. Had they studied the history of the "Great Game" in Afghanistan in the nineteenth century and of the Russian attempt to conquer the country in the 1980s; had they familiarised themselves with the complex history of Iraq and the disastrous British military involvement there in the early twentieth century, they might have proceeded more cautiously. It certainly seems to be true that neither Bush nor Blair had any knowledge of, or interest in, the history of either country when the decision to invade was agreed on – despite George Bush claiming that history books are among his favourite reading.

It is doubtful, however, how much people can learn from history. History is not a neutral discipline like one of the pure sciences. It is biased by the national tradition of the historian, by his language, and by fashionable academic theory. History does not belong only to historians, either; politicians frequently seize on it and manipulate it, so that a proposed course of action is presented as the fulfilment of a country's historical role. In this way, the American version of national history, which is bound up in the concept of "Manifest Destiny" – itself a mish-mash of the ancient appeal to the will of God, armed might and imperial ambition – can be used by an aggressive conservative like George W. Bush to justify dealing death to hundreds of thousands of people. History is there to be used and misused by politicians and by nations in the furtherance of their own ambitions. "History", in this sense, is part of the deep structure of history itself as academic historians understand it.

There is a further problem with the notion of learning from history, which is related to evolved aspects of human nature.

Every generation of young men appears to have an innate need to test itself under extreme conditions. Many societies have *rites de passage* in which young warriors can prove themselves in the face of danger. In societies that have abandoned the practice, such as the industrialised societies of the West, males on the verge of adulthood seek out alternatives in, for example, the current fashion for extreme sports, or in random violence on the streets. Gang membership should be seen, in part, as an urban equivalent to the elite band of young warriors in tribal society, and gang violence as part of an unconscious attempt to recreate the *rite de passage*. The problem of course is that instead of inducting young men into the adult world, gang violence places them beyond the law, so they become pariahs circling society's edge.

The existence in each generation of such a cohort means that political leaders with aggressive ambitions have to hand an ever ready human resource for waging war. It is known that armies thrive on recruits between the ages of eighteen and twenty-one, because compared even with slightly older men, it is easier to get them to kill. The ground for war has to be prepared, often by appealing to a version of national history and destiny; but once this is done, gambling everything on military aggression can seem an attractive course of action to a certain kind of politician, as it did to George W. Bush, and as it did to Tony Blair.

It is rare to find a political leader like Dwight D. Eisenhower who warned against the consequences of developing a massive industrial-military complex of the kind that now dominates the United States. Eisenhower's own experience of the devastation of the Second World War certainly influenced his thinking. It is the fact that it *did* influence him against war as an instrument of policy, other than as a last resort, which is so impressive and unusual. Rather, in each generation, leaders emerge who convince themselves that war is an easy and valid instrument of policy, that they are not gambling, and that the outcome of war is not necessarily grim for victors and losers alike. Almost always, they find people eager to listen.

Jehovah's Witnesses who come to the door are fond of quoting Jesus' words to the disciples in Matthew 24: 6-8:

And ye shall hear of wars and rumours of wars: see that ye be not troubled: for all these things must come to pass, but the end is not yet.

For nation shall rise against nation, and kingdom against kingdom: and there shall be famines, and pestilences, and earthquakes, in divers places.

All these are the beginning of sorrows.

To the Witnesses, this is a tribute to the power of prophecy. See, they say, this is exactly what is happening now. But the beginning of sorrows was a long time before Jesus spoke, deep in human prehistory, and there is no sign of it ending.

MAPS

In March 2005 I was invited by the Israeli Information Centre in Cardiff, along with three other Welsh people, to go on a fact finding visit to Israel. The purpose, I was told, was to provide a more balanced view of the country and so help counter the alleged anti-Israeli bias of the Welsh media. It turned out to be a very intense four days in which we met, among others, diplomats (including a former ambassador to Britain), an officer from the IDF, academics from the Hebrew University, and a Palestinian journalist who specialised in reporting Palestinian Authority corruption for an Israeli newspaper. We were told that we might also meet someone from the Peace Movement, a member of the Knesset and someone from the Palestinian Authority if a visa could be arranged, but in the end these meetings did not occur.

I thought a great deal about that visit, and how I might write about it for *Planet* which I edited at the time. I never seemed able to find an angle, however – a way in to the profusion of arguments, positions, voices, as well as the visits, to Yad Vashem, the Western Wall, the Intifada Museum, the Church of Saint John the Baptist, a hospital that cared for poor children with heart damage from around the world, the separation barrier, an international relief agency – until the Israeli invasion of Lebanon in 2006, which sharpened suddenly the focus on what I had seen and heard.

Looking back, my visit seems to have been based on maps – political maps that told truths and maps that told lies; maps that revealed truths they weren't designed to show. In advance of the visit, we were given information material which included *The Arab-Israeli Conflict in Maps*. The first four maps in this booklet, under the heading "Periods of Jewish independence", were of the unintentionally revealing kind. Map 1 showed the Kingdom of David and Solomon in the tenth century BC, Maps 2 and 3 the fluctuating borders of the Divided Kingdom of the tenth to sixth centuries BC and the Hasmonean Kingdom of the first century BC. Map 4 showed "Israel within the boundaries and ceasefire lines, 1991" (the booklet was published that year). On this, there is no Gaza and no West Bank; Israel stretches seamlessly from the Mediterranean to the Dead Sea, from Elat to the Golan Heights. For convenience, the borders of Map 4 are superimposed on the other three. Give or take part of Jordan north and east of the Dead Sea, the Kingdom of David and Solomon is contiguous with the "Greater Israel" of the 1991 map.

Then there was the Intifada Museum in Tel Aviv. That was a gruesome place with displays of homemade rockets, tailor's dummies with robes opened to reveal belts packed with explosives and studded with ball-bearings for maximum damage. There were photographs, one of a street shortly after a suicide bombing, strewn with glass and rubble, and in the middle of the road the leg of what moments before would have been a burly man, naked and frayed where it had been torn away at the hip – as if it had fallen from a passing butcher's van. And again there were maps.

These had been pasted onto a series of recessed sliding panels. The young woman who showed us around, slid them one by one into view. They were political maps too, but this time PLO maps that ignored the existence of Israel. She stopped and explicated some maps while others were briefly shown then slid aside. One of these had hundreds of blue dots marked on it. What were those? one of our party asked. She slid the map back. "Oh these are the Arab villages that were destroyed in 1948."

At the Hebrew University in Jerusalem we were lectured on the proposed route of the "separation barrier". Again there were maps, one showing the Israeli settlements in the West Bank. Later, looking at the map with our Israeli guide, I asked about what seemed a very isolated settlement, way out on its own. Why is that one there? "That's where the prophet So-and-So was born", was the answer.

The demography of the region – which has much to do with maps – was a preoccupation of many of the experts we met. Pains were taken to emphasise that Israel is a bi-national state, with Arab citizens, and that a substantial number of foreign nationals live and work there as well; but again and again the lecture or dinner-table conversation turned to the "demographic time-bomb" caused by the differential birth rates of Israeli Jews and Arabs. We were assured that Arab families were consistently larger than Jewish ones, partly because Arab men often take more than one wife. (When I mentioned this at dinner to a Christian Israeli Arab, a lecturer in law at the Hebrew University, he reacted angrily – "That's crap," he said. "That's cheap propaganda.") In this context, we were presented with the "problem" of the West Bank. If it ever became part of the Israeli state and Palestinians had voting rights, Jews, we were told, would be outvoted in the Knesset within a couple of decades, becoming a minority in their own country. This is why Palestinian refugees from the war of 1948, and their descendants, can never have the right of return of the kind that all Jews have, wherever they are in the world. Despite this, Israel is a democracy, we were assured, and the only one in the Middle East. Whether it is a democracy for Jews or a multi-racial one, however, remained unclear and seemed indeed a fluid concept, depending on what stage the conversation had reached. The fact that Arab Israelis are in effect second-class citizens, with curtailed rights, was never put into words.

Many ghosts lay behind these arguments. Several times we had quoted at us the old Zionist slogan that Palestine had been "A land without a people, for a people without a land". But that was never true. In 1947 there were in fact approximately 1.2 million Arabs in Palestine, 711,000 of whom, according to UN estimates, either fled or were forcibly removed or emigrated during the 1948 war, when the UN-mandated state was rejected by the Arab states. Yet in Israeli propaganda, these people are presented as being historically stateless. There is no such thing as a "Palestinian", we were assured, because there has never been a Palestinian state. In a technical sense this may be true, yet before 1948 there had been no Jewish state either for two thousand years. In such historical circumstances, what gives one people an inalienable right to the land and another people, already living there, no right at all?

One answer takes us into the realm of religion – Canaan/Israel is the Promised Land, promised by God to Abraham and his descendants in perpetuity in Genesis. Hence the juxtaposition of the Kingdom of David and Solomon with Israel within the 1991 "borders" as defined in *The Arab-Israeli Conflict in Maps*. Hence too in later maps in the booklet the labelling of the West Bank as "Samaria" and "Judea". Maps, their meanings; passed over by the ignorant, brooded on by the knowing.

Christian Zionists in America and elsewhere also find such religious determinism congenial – for them, too, the establishment of the state of Israel in 1948 is in accordance with biblical prophecy; the land is God-given. There is another justification for Israeli expansion at the expense of the Palestinian Arabs, however, which is rarely expressed directly, though we caught more than a whiff of it in our fours days in Israel. It is that Arabs are an inferior "race".

This is not just a Jewish Israeli thought. It underlay British attitudes in the Middle East during and after the First World War, and it informed American policy in occupied Iraq where US forces consistently refused to count Iraqi dead, because – though of course again it is never said out loud – Arab lives are cheap compared with Western lives. Three thousand died in the Twin Towers, tens of thousands died in Iraq in a trumped-up invasion. (Thousands of Afghans died in Afghanistan too, and are still dying, but they also have not been counted, and in the West are easily forgotten.)

In Israel, the same rule of thumb applies. During the 2006 invasion of Lebanon, it is estimated that at least a thousand Lebanese were killed, many of them civilians, including children. The Israeli death toll was 119 IDF soldiers and 43 civilians, the latter killed in rocket attacks on Israel. During the invasion of Gaza in 2008-09 the disparity in the casualty figures is even more striking. The total number of Gazans killed is disputed, though not by that much. The Palestinian Ministry of Health estimates that 1324 were killed, most of whom were civilians. The Palestinian Centre for Human Rights puts the death toll at 1285, including 895 civilians. The Israeli Defence Force figure is 1200, of whom 300 were non-combatant women, children under 15 and men over 65. This means that the IDF identified any male between the ages of 15 and 65 as a Hamas militant, and therefore a legitimate target. The Israeli death toll, according to Israeli sources, was 13; 10 IDF soldiers and 3 civilians.

These figures are similar to the ratio of 1 to 100 used by the SS and the Werhmacht in parts of occupied Europe when exacting revenge for the death of a German soldier killed by partisans or resistance fighters. It is difficult not to see the savage invasion of Gaza in a similar light, as a punitive expedition, a revenge attack conducted on the pretext that it was necessary to stop Hamas from launching rockets into southern Israel. It was not Hamas, however, who had broken the previous cease-fire, but the Israelis when they crossed the Gazan border and killed 6 Hamas fighters. Only then did the rocket attacks start again.

In the aftermath of the invasion, the dissident Israeli historian, Ilan Pappe, has argued that Israel has no interest in peace, and no intention of negotiating a settlement that would involve the creation of a viable Palestinian state. The main thrust of Israeli policy, he suggests, has always been, and is now, the creation of a Greater Israel based on the biblical kingdom of David and Solomon. In such a state there would be no place for the Palestinians who must be cowed into accepting existence in what he terms the world's largest open-air prison. It is hard not to see Gaza as the blueprint for that prison.

In the *London Review of Books*, *Haaretz* journalist, Amira Hass, reported on what she saw when she visited Gaza after the IDF withdrew in 2009. Many houses occupied by IDF troops during the invasion had been deliberately wrecked, furniture smashed, the walls smeared with excrement, and defaced with graffiti. "The Zionist conqueror was here," read one graffito in Hebrew. "We're here to annihilate you," read another. In some cases, houses were dynamited as the IDF withdrew.

When Arab civilians are killed, as they are all the time in this endless conflict, it is "collateral damage". If enough are killed, there is an official Israeli expression of "regret" with a cynical shrug of the shoulders. Stuff, as Donald Rumsfeld said, happens.

During our stay in Israel, we were assured time and again that the IDF only responds to attacks on Israel and that military response is always proportionate. Israel is always the innocent party, always provoked. And Israeli civilians who died horribly in the First and Second Intifadas *were* innocent; certainly the teenage girl was who died in the pizza parlour suicide bombing in Jerusalem, whose father we met during our visit.

But Israel the state is not innocent. Beneath its foundations lies the rubble of Arab farms and villages; beyond its borders are the old people and their descendants, holding the keys to doors that no longer exist, the deeds to land that is theirs by right of laws that have been abrogated by the conqueror. The men and women who joined the PLO, who voted democratically for Hamas, who cheered Hizbollah's semi-victory in south Lebanon, have their claims in God-given Canaan, Samaria and Judea, too, though they have other names for those places. But slowly and surely, Israel is creating Greater Israel out of the West Bank with its network of settlements and fortifications, its caging of the Palestinians in powerless bantustans that can breed only frustration, hatred and more violence. How long can Israel go on seeing itself always as the innocent victim, never the aggressor?

On our first day in Jerusalem, after booking into the hotel and a quick breakfast, we were taken to Yad Vashem, the Holocaust museum and memorial. Apart from ourselves at that early hour, the museum's rooms were packed with young IDF recruits in battle dress, automatic rifles slung over their shoulders, being lectured by their officers. We followed them through room after room of photographs from the ghettos and the concentration camps; a black-and-white world of silence and horror, and the shame of humanity. *Never again*, must have been the Hebrew message of the officers to the recruits staring at the photographs. *To be safe is to be strong.* But what is strength without compassion? And what if strength alone, translated into collective punishment in Gaza and the West Bank, and Lebanon — what if strength does not and cannot buy the peace Israel desires? What if, looking at the hollow eyes in the Warsaw ghetto, you are also looking into the eyes of the slaughtered at Chatila, into the eyes of the dead children at Qana?

Somehow Israel needs to come to terms with the truth about its foundation and its policies since 1967; and to act on the discomfiting self-knowledge which awareness of the truth brings. It cannot rely on strength alone, for strength which is expressed in a brutal militarism that involves crimes against the international laws of war will end by destroying Israel, not from without, but morally from within.

BARACK OBAMA

In the early stages of the long and exhausting American presidential campaign in 2008, Barack Obama seemed a rank outsider,
one of those promising politicians who declare their candidature
only to withdraw it after a few weeks or months. Obama, it was
said, was too young, too lacking in experience of high-level
politics, and he was Black. There could be no competition with
Hilary Clinton, a seasoned campaigner with an established power
base, especially among women voters.

Hilary Clinton must have thought so too at the beginning of
the campaign for the Democratic nomination, but as Barack
Obama's qualities became apparent to an increasingly apprecia-
tive public, her team was forced to step up the attack on him in
what became, toward the end, a desperate and sometimes
rancorous attempt to undermine his avalanching popularity.

It didn't work, as we know, any more than the attempt by the
McCain-Palin team to rubbish his character and political credentials during the presidential campaign itself. For Barack Obama is
a politician of a kind that has not been seen in Western politics for
a generation or more, so much so that there has been a danger of
regarding him as somehow unique.

From the beginning, he rejected a campaign based on muck-
raking which is one of the most unattractive features of American
politics and when attacked himself he remained unruffled, refusing to be drawn. It must have been frustrating to someone like
Sarah Palin for whom cheap shots were the only shots she had.

Then again, unlike his opponents, he was articulate. When
asked a question, he thought about it before giving a measured

answer in clear, concise sentences. There was no danger of misunderestimating him. So articulate is Barack Obama, in fact, that he was compared in the American press to Cicero, with articles analysing his speeches in terms of the tropes of Classical rhetoric. Without denigrating Obama's eloquence, this says more about the dismal state of political oratory in the Western democracies than it does about the man.

Moreover, there is no need to go to the Ancient world for comparisons, for there is a precedent much closer to home, and one which Obama himself has acknowledged – Abraham Lincoln. In an allusion to his Ohio connection with his great nineteenth century predecessor, Obama launched his own bid for the presidency in Springfield, Ohio, as Lincoln did nearly a hundred and fifty years ago. Two days before his inauguration, he cemented the association by giving a speech at the Lincoln Memorial, with the statue of the seated president, deep in thought, looking down on him. That day, 18 January, was also the eve of Martin Luther King's birthday, another thoughtful, articulate and humane politician with whom Obama sought association.

While George W. Bush, who professes an interest in history, sat about by his own account, reading books like *Grunts*, Barack Obama showed from the beginning a subtle sense of American history and how it could be used to make a statement about his aspirations and intentions. In almost anyone else, this symbolic appropriation of the mantles of Lincoln and King would have seemed, at best, hubristic, and at worst the ploy of a cynical politician. That it did not seem so in Obama's case, is a measure of the gravitas he had achieved by the time of his inauguration.

Barack Obama is certainly the West's best hope as we enter the second decade of the twenty-first century, yet even with his considerable abilities, it is a question of how much he can achieve, given the multiple crises the world is embroiled in and the opposition he faces in the United States from hardcore conservative opponents who rapidly regrouped after the shock of defeat. It is worth remembering that 47 per cent of those who voted, voted for John McCain and Sarah Palin, despite the fact that McCain's age and health problems meant there was a good chance that Palin would succeed him as president, and despite her revealing during the campaign how ignorant, uneducated, petty minded, and abusive she was. Sarah Palin may have shot her bolt as far as the highest offices in American politics are concerned, but she is still someone to be reckoned with at the grassroots level – as her popularity with the Tea Party movement makes clear. Meanwhile, Barack Obama has become a figure of hate for right-wing radio commentators like Rush Limbaugh and their considerable following, and that hatred is likely to increase with time.

Obama's domestic programme as President is far reaching, immensely ambitious and, in American terms, some way to the left. The international financial and banking crisis which began in the United States, and the ensuing deep recession, gave him, or so he gambled, the opportunity to introduce reforms that would address the economic and social inequalities that are endemic in America. What he proposed was something akin to Franklin D. Roosevelt's New Deal, involving substantial government spending and dirigiste policies that are counter in every way to the neo-conservative ideology of the Bush regime and to the strongly held beliefs of a large section of the electorate. Foremost among his declared policies was a bill to create universal health insurance, to be paid for in part by abolishing George W. Bush's tax concessions to the richest 5 per cent, and by increasing taxation on families earning over $250,000. The plan came up against such determined opposition in Congress and the Senate, however, as well as more generally from large, vocal sectors of the electorate, that it had to be reduced in scope. Nonetheless, when the revised proposals were narrowly passed by Congress at the end of March 2010, it was a signal triumph for Obama.

As could have been predicted, however, the president failed to make any headway in persuading Republicans in either house to support the health insurance bill, and his appeal, during his first months in office, for a cross-party consensus in the face of the multiple crises facing America, seems naive in retrospect, the product of a liberal, inclusive idealism that had no chance of making headway against the belligerent ideology-laden convictions of his opponents. The Republicans, in fact, closed ranks in preparation for a long-drawn out confrontation with his administration.

When it came to foreign affairs, Obama indicated that here too he would initiate a radically different set of policies, declaring an end to the brute-force approach of the Bush era and a return to traditional diplomacy and multilateralism. This bore fruit in 2010 in an agreement with Russia on the limitation of Russian and American nuclear arsenals to 1500 bombs each (tactical nuclear weapons were not included). Elsewhere, however, his initiatives have been less successful.

In his early forays into foreign affairs in 2009 it was perhaps too easy to be charmed by his oratory. Regarding Iran, Barack Obama's tone was firm but conciliatory: "…if countries like Iran are willing to unclench their fist," he said, "they will find an extended hand from us." This is welcome after Bush's demonization of Iran as part of an apocalyptic "Axis of Evil"; it is nonetheless a sleight of hand, as if America has been the peacemaker in the Middle East all along. As Hasan Ghashghavi, a spokesman for the Iranian Foreign Ministry, responded, "If there is any clenched fist in the world, it is the fist of the USA."

From the beginning of his presidency, Obama made it clear that he intended to right some of the worst foreign policy excesses of the Bush administration, promising to close Guantánamo by the end of his first year in office, for example, and making a commitment to the withdrawal of US forces from Iraq. At the same time, however, he continued the Bush administration's policy in Afghanistan in the apparent belief that the war against the Taliban could be won given a sufficiently large military presence. In war nothing is certain, of course, but historical precedents are not promising. Neither the British in the nineteenth century, nor the Russians in the twentieth, were able to control, let alone govern, Afghanistan. The inhospitable terrain, the porous border with the semi-autonomous tribal regions of north-west Pakistan, the long supply lines facing any invading force, and the fact that Taliban fighters are among the best guerillas in the world operating in a harsh environment which they know intimately, make victory for the Americans (and an increasingly reluctant NATO force) unlikely. After all, despite a decade of intensive searching, the Americans have not even been able to locate and capture Osama bin Laden, the original casus belli.

An unintended consequence of the Bush-Obama war against

the Taliban has been increased instability in Pakistan, large swathes of which have passed into extremist Islamist hands and are beyond effective government control. The collapse of a nuclear, and more or less secular, Pakistan would be the worst possible outcome with consequences across the region.

Moreover, a protracted war against Islamists in Afghanistan – with the all too familiar reports of heavy civilian casualties that would be unacceptable if Afghans were Westerners – is unlikely to persuade countries like Iran that America is extending the hand of conciliation.

The same may be said of Obama's silence during Israel's invasion of Gaza in 2008-09, despite the ferocity of the IDF's attack and its lack of all proportion. It can be argued that since the invasion occurred before his inauguration, Obama felt unable to comment. This did not, however, prevent the president-elect from intervening forcefully during the financial crisis. Perhaps the Obama administration may yet surprise the world with a more vigorous and even-handed diplomacy which presses the case for Palestinian independence, in return for recognition of the Israeli state as defined by its pre-1967 borders. In a lecture at the Department of International Politics in Aberystwyth in January 2009, however, Ilan Pappe was pessimistic. It would, he suggested, be business as usual.

Events during the first year and a half of the presidency would seem to confirm this. Early on, Obama made a bold speech in Cairo promising a more even-handed American policy in the Middle East. It was the kind of speech that had endeared him to liberals at home and throughout Europe. Yet, well into the second year of his presidency, as I write, little or nothing has changed. For though the administration has taken a public stand against further Israeli settlement in the West Bank, each time the issue is raised Netanyahu gives Obama the cold stare and goes on building.

In March 2010, when Vice-President Joe Biden was in Jerusalem to negotiate an agreement on indirect talks between Israel and Palestine, Netanyahu's government announced plans to build 1600 new houses in an Orthodox Jewish quarter of occupied East Jerusalem, which is claimed by the Palestinians as the capital of any future independent state. A few hours before the announcement, Biden had reaffirmed the Obama administration's "absolute, total and unvarnished" commitment to Israel. In the ensuing furore, Netanyahu claimed that the timing of the announcement had been an unfortunate administrative error, adding that the proposed housing project would nonetheless take place. Such an "apology" only added insult to the original announcement. The housing scheme was condemned in harsh terms for an American administration, but this was immediately undermined by Hilary Clinton, the Secretary of State, who assured Israel of America's continued commitment to its security. That is all Netanyahu needed to know.

It is hard to believe that the timing of the announcement of the new housing project was accidental. It has been clear for a long time that successive Israeli governments have had no interest in a two-state solution to the Palestinian problem. Since 1967 Israel has set as its goal the creation of Greater Israel, through settlement of the West Bank, squeezing the Arab population into impoverished enclaves. As several commentators have observed, Israel is turning itself into an Apartheid state.

The question is why, after the noble speeches of intent, Obama has so far done nothing to discourage Israel from this course; just as he has failed, at the time of writing, to make good his election promise to close Guantánamo which he rightly saw as an enduring stain on America's reputation.

Those who suggested that, articulate and intelligent as he is, Obama came to the presidency lacking in sufficient experience of high-level politics may have had a point. It is beginning to seem as if this may be true and that, combined with the poisonous inheritance of the Bush years, he is not going to be able to make good many of the promises on which he was elected. As far as Israel is concerned, he almost certainly underestimated the power of the Jewish lobby in America, as well as the generally unquestioning support for Israel that exists in Congress and the Senate. Like Israeli prime ministers before him, Netanyahu knows this and knows that all he has to do is bide his time. The American right certainly suffered a set-back in the election defeat of 2008, but it may well have been little more than that and Obama may not see a second term in office.

There is time yet for momentous events before the next presidential election, but if Barack Obama fails, it may be precisely where so many other US presidents have failed, in the field of foreign policy. More decisive here than failure to negotiate a just settlement of the Israeli-Palestinian conflict may be Obama's decision to continue and expand Bush's war in Afghanistan. Perhaps again this was forced on him, for no US president can afford to appear soft on Islamic terrorism, even though it is clear that the war against the Taliban has actually increased the terrorist threat and is a war like Vietnam which America is unlikely to win.

Adam Shatz made a pertinent comment in the *London Review of Books* in February 2009. "He might," he wrote of Obama, "remember the example of Lyndon Johnson, who presided over the most ambitious programme of civil rights and anti-poverty legislation ever launched in the US, while pursuing a murderous, wasteful war that for ever stained his presidency."

If the Obama presidency fails, or is perceived to have failed in the eyes of the American public, then it is likely to open the door to a prolonged period of right-wing government that will have fateful consequences for the United States and the rest of the world.

THE SOUL

I have never heard it asked of a Christian: when did humans acquire a soul? If you are a Creationist of course the answer is easy: humankind acquired its soul when God created man and woman on the sixth day, as revealed in Genesis. There is no arguing with such a position. If you are a liberal Christian, though, who rejects biblical literalism and accepts the theory of evolution, the question becomes more difficult.

Anatomically modern humans emerged some 200,000 years ago. But at that time, *Homo sapiens* was not the only human species on Earth. An ancestor species, *Homo erectus*, still existed in China and South-East Asia where it had spread from East Africa, surviving in Java until perhaps 27,000 years ago; and from about 190,000 to at least 30,000 years ago a species closely related to us, the Neanderthals, lived in Europe and periodically in the Near East, adapted to the harsh conditions of the last Ice Age.

Homo erectus had a much smaller brain than ourselves and it is generally agreed among palaeoanthropologists that it did not have the capacity for speech as we understand it. Yet there is evidence that it shared what we would consider distinctly human traits such as caring for the chronically sick.

Homo neanderthalensis had a brain that was larger than ours, if organised slightly differently. The Neanderthals deliberately buried their dead, though it is disputed as to whether this had any significance other than waste disposal. They almost certainly had some form of speech. The relative positions of the larynx, pharynx, tongue and hyoid bone, however, suggest that they may not have been capable of fully articulated speech in our sense.

Toward the end of their existence in the far West of Europe there is evidence of cultural contact with *Homo sapiens* in the form of copies made by Neanderthals of human artefacts.

If we were to meet a Neanderthal or even a *Homo erectus*, we would find them physically like us in many ways. Yet would we call them human, or would we put them in a zoo? DNA, recently extracted from Neanderthal skeletons, suggests that *Homo sapiens* at times interbred with Neanderthals who are probably a distinct, though closely related, species. Their fate is disputed. What is known is that as anatomically modern humans emerged out of Africa into the Near East and Eastern and Central Europe, the Neanderthals appear to have been driven West, the last known survivors eking out a living on the western coast of Spain 30,000 years ago.

Palaeoanthropologists have suggested various reasons for what seems to be the progressive supplanting of the Neanderthals by humans. Superior technology and more complex social organisation, it is argued, would have given humans an advantage in hunting and gathering, which in turn would have enabled them to produce more offspring and so in effect outbreed the Neanderthals. Humans, too, may have been quicker to adapt to changing climatic conditions; Neanderthals may have been more conservative in their habits and lost out when climate change caused a geographical redistribution of their preferred prey.

No palaeontologist I have read has been willing to speculate that, perhaps, when early humans made first contact with Neanderthals (and with the surviving *Homo erectus* populations in China and South-East Asia) they may also have killed them off. Given what we know about the history of first contact between Europeans and the Native Americans of North and South America, or the Aborigines of Australia, this seems a highly plausible scenario, yet palaeontologists shy away from it even as a contributory factor in the extinction of these species.

The reason, I suspect, has little to do with the evidence (in fact there is almost none, one way or the other) and a lot to do with contemporary susceptibilities. In recent decades, the white populations of Europe, Australia and North America have been led to a painful reckoning with their colonial past and the genocides it produced. On top of this, there are the millions on millions killed in the twentieth century in two world wars, in the Nazi death camps, in the Soviet gulags, in the famines caused by Soviet collectivisation and the famines caused by Mao's Cultural Revolution, to name only the worst. It is hard not to see our species in the twentieth century other than through the grim image of Goya's *Saturn Devouring One of His Sons*.

If early humans did kill off the Neanderthals, however, as they expanded across Europe, and the last populations of *Homo erectus* as they moved into Asia, then it would suggest that our species had a murderous tendency from the beginning, and that what happened over the past one hundred years was not a terrible aberration, but an expression of a deeply rooted aspect of human nature which, given the right conditions, will manifest itself again and again. Palaeoanthropologists, like a lot of people, are reluctant to embrace this view of humanity.

Moreover, the more palaeoanthropologists discover about the hominid species who once shared the Earth with us, the more sympathetic and human they become. If we still tend to limit the adjective *human* to our own species, it is because for thousands of years we believed our species to be unique. The discoveries of palaeoanthropology during the past one hundred and fifty years have thrown that uniqueness in doubt. Perhaps we should use the word *human* about Neanderthals too, and even *Homo erectus* who would have looked so like us. If we do, however, we de-centre ourselves, as if, on looking in the mirror of time, we see ourselves, the humans, with different humans who we may have extermi-nated peering over our shoulders.

And this brings us back to the question: if the soul exists, as Christianity says it does, when did it manifest itself in human beings? It might be argued that this took place 200,000 years ago when anatomically modern humans emerged for the first time and the human population was a tiny 10,000 or so individuals limited to East Africa. In this case, you might expect early archae-ological sites to reveal evidence of religious ritual, but for the first 100,000 years of our species' existence no such evidence has so far been found. From about 100,000 years ago humans began to bury their dead but the graves excavated so far do not indicate ritual burial of a kind which would imply the presence of religious belief. Like the Neanderthals and *Homo erectus*, early humans may well have lived without religion. Only after the extraordinary cultural explosion that occurred some 50,000 years ago is there unequivocal evidence of ritual burial with religious implications.

A more subtle answer might be that the soul was *emergent* over a period of time, and that its full expression was dependent on the evolution of a modern language-dominated consciousness. The danger of this line of argument, for the Christian, is that the soul can be interpreted merely as a primitive (in the sense of early) attempt to grapple with the phenomenon of consciousness, and that "soul" is merely a synonym for consciousness.

In a sense, the Creationists are right to insist on the literal interpretation of the Bible. For once it is conceded that Genesis and other biblical texts are myth, the truth as Christians have perceived it for 2000 years begins to slip and slide, ending in the evasions and pseudo-profundities of the untenanted cross and the *Deus absconditus*. If the Earth is 4.8 billion years old, for example, and was not created in 4004 BC, as many Creationists believe; if species are not the static products of a single Creation, but have evolved over hundreds of millions of years, with more species having become extinct than are currently living; and if humans are not a unique creation, but an evolved species of the genus *Homo* that includes ancestor and collateral species – then you have to start asking questions about God and the nature of life all over again, and this time looking closely at the evidence provided by the material universe, rather than relying on the word of God said to have been "revealed" in Near Eastern agricultural communities 2000 to 2500 years ago.

A divine plan for humanity, for example, comes to seem more than a little absurd. Were the Neanderthals and *Homo erectus*, with all their human and yet not-quite-human attributes, merely bad try-outs, inferior models that God experimented with and abandoned? Perhaps because of the limited capacity, or the arrangement, of their brains they did not have souls, in which case they could neither be saved nor damned? *Homo erectus* was nonetheless around for almost 1.8 million years; a considerably longer span of time than ourselves to date.

Let's concede that only members of our own species, *Homo sapiens*, have souls. The question remains: when was it breathed into our bodies? For there is no clear-cut division, physically, between very early humans and *Homo erectus*; rather there is a slow emergence of one from the other, with intermediary skeletons containing attributes of both.

Then again, there is the question of salvation. Our species existed for 200,000 years before God sent his son in the form of a man, to preach salvation to humanity. Medieval theologians were aware of the problem this poses: were all those who lived and died before the Incarnation – and so before they had a chance to hear God's Word as revealed through Jesus – irrevocably condemned to burn in Hell? This would seem logical but it cuts across the idea of God as a God of Love. So the doctrine of the good pagan was developed, whereby men and women who lived according to the best of moral precepts before Jesus came to Earth, would be absolved of their sins and enter Heaven after a suitable period in Purgatory.

Theologians in the Middle Ages had of course no idea of the true age of the Earth, or of the true age of humanity, or of the fact that other species of humans have existed before and coterminous with ourselves. The vast majority of the generations of humankind lived and died before the Incarnation and never heard the Gospel. Purgatory must be very capacious.

We can take this further. The vast majority of humans who lived and died in the past 2000 years were never exposed to the Gospel either. This being so, it becomes reasonable to ask what God has been up to; why the Incarnation took place so late in human history; why Jesus was born into a minor Near Eastern province of the Roman Empire so that the millions of sub-Saharan Africa, North and South America, Australasia, Polynesia, China and Central Asia had to wait another 1500 years until European missionaries began to spread God's Word among them. The Christian version of the broad sweep of human history begins to look sloppy. It raises more questions than it provides answers; it stumbles again and again against the hard evidence produced by the human, biological and geophysical sciences.

A Christian might answer with St Paul: "…now we see

through a glass, darkly; but then face to face: now I know in part; but then shall I know even as also I am known." It is the age-old evasion of religion in the face of uncomfortable facts – the deaths of children from disease; the random deaths of tens of thousands in natural disasters. We cannot know God's mind, is the argument; what seems inexplicable and even unconscionable to us now will be understood when we stand before the Throne, when we see face to face. For God is Love and the trials He subjects humanity to are an expression of that love, even though we cannot always fathom His purpose, gazing into the mirror of our earthly existence.

Some scientists, most notably the evolutionary biologist Stephen Jay Gould, have tried to shrug off issues of religion by arguing that science and religion inhabit two separate domains, science being concerned with the material universe which can be measured and with theories which can be falsified, while religion pronounces on a non-material world which cannot be measured in scientific terms, and with claims to truth based on revelation which cannot be falsified. These domains, so Gould has argued, do not overlap and so cannot be in conflict with one another.

This proposition would be convenient if it were true, but it ignores the fact that Christianity has always made statements about the nature of the material universe of a kind which are falsifiable and which inevitably bring it on a collision course with science. Charles Darwin was aware of this and was reluctant for many years to publish his theory of the evolution of species by natural selection because he realised that it had profound religious, philosophical and social implications. It is the reason why Creationists and Intelligent Designers are so vehemently opposed to Darwinism, and why the Papacy only recently conceded that evolutionary theory expressed a true understanding of how species evolve, though with the qualification that the theory can say nothing about the origins of life or our ultimate end. This, however, is a bit of evasive face-saving. Evolutionary biology, biochemistry and cosmology between them have a lot to say about the origin of life and its probable end. It is true that, because the one belongs to the remotest beginnings of the universe and the other to an inconceivably far off time in the universe's future, scientists may never be able to produce falsifiable theories about them. However, hypotheses deduced from what we can observe are at least as likely to be near the truth as the Word of God revealed to early agriculturalists, whose understanding of the nature of the universe has in almost every respect been superseded. Christianity, along with most other religions, is a pre-scientific attempt to explain who we are, how we came to be here, and how the material universe was created and what its purpose is.

Christianity, taking the Old and New Testaments together, is a powerful expression of human curiosity, fear and hope; a recognition of how small we are before the vastness of the universe; of the brief nature of our existence; of our sense of the uniqueness of individual consciousness; and of the fact that, unlike the other animals, we know we must die. Historically, Christianity has held out the promise of salvation and damnation in equal measure, but most of all it has proclaimed that death is not the end, that some immaterial part of ourselves will survive the body's decay to see "face to face".

This vision of humankind and the universe, once so dominant, has been challenged inadvertently by science and is in a state of crisis. Christians have responded in one of two ways. Literalists have denied the science, especially what seems to them the iniquitous theory of evolution which they rightly see as undermining the authority of the Bible. They have either simply held firm to biblical literalism as Creationists, or they have attempted to challenge evolutionary theory on its own terms through the promotion of a counter theory of Intelligent Design. This purports to investigate life on Earth with scientific rigour, proving that species are and can only be the product of an intelligent designer, which is to say, God. Intelligent Design is not even bad science, it is cod-science, but this has not prevented it being highly influential among literalist Christians in the United States, with political implications for the state funding of the biological sciences and the way they are taught in schools and colleges under administrations like that of George W. Bush.

The other response, among moderates and Protestant Christian intellectuals, has been to accept some version of

Gould's pact between religion and science, acknowledging that Christianity's domain is the "spiritual" and the ethical. Under these conditions, the Virgin Birth, the Incarnation and the Resurrection are all up for reinterpretation as symbol or metaphor, and God retreats from the material universe, becoming the paradoxical, elusive Deus absconditus.

As Edward O. Wilson has written, it is probable that the religious impulse is a hard-wired attribute of humans, a by-product of our enlarged brains and the emergence of consciousness. If this is so, then no amount of evidence adduced by science, which suggests we are a fleeting insignificant part of a vast material universe with no discernible teleology, will have any lasting effect on human faith in religion. Science can lead us in the direction of a rational contemplation of human nature but it cannot offer us any consolation for the human condition. Christianity offers us God's love, immortality, and a place in Heaven if we live by His precepts on Earth. We are small, it says, but no detail is too small in the eyes of God, for "Are not two sparrows sold for a farthing? And one of them shall not fall on the ground without your Father. But the very hairs of your head are numbered. Fear ye not therefore, ye are of more value than many sparrows."

When, like the last Neanderthals, the last humans gather together – whenever that may be – the likelihood is that it will be in a dusky church, temple, synagogue or mosque, and that their last words will be prayers to the God of Sparrows, for the salvation of those will-o'-the-wisps, their souls.

THE BOOK OF REVELATION

The Revelation of St John the Divine, the last book of the New Testament and the last book of the Bible, is one of the most extraordinary works ever written. It purports to be the revelation of Christ himself to John, but a Christ transformed who has cast off the human form he used to reveal God's word in the Gospels. "I am Alpha and Omega, the beginning and the ending," says a voice, and when John turns to see who it is, he is confronted by seven golden candlesticks in the midst of which is a figure "like unto the Son of man", except that

> His head and his hairs were white like wool, as white as snow; and his eyes were as a flame of fire;
> And his feet like unto fine brass, as if they burned in a furnace; and his voice as the sound of many waters.
> And he had in his right hand seven stars: and out of his mouth went a sharp twoedged sword: and his countenance was as the sun shineth in his strength.

If this Christ is the son of anybody it quickly becomes apparent that it is Yahweh, the vengeful god of the Old Testament who harbours grudges and hatreds that are never too small to be remembered. Christ begins by giving an account of the virtues and shortcomings of the "seven churches". Each is praised, though each is found wanting. "But this thou hast," he says in a consolatory manner, addressing the church of Ephesus, "that thou hatest the deeds of the Nicolaitans, which I also hate." The church in Pergamos, on the contrary, harbours some who "hold the doctrine of the Nicolaitans, which thing I hate".

It is good for the congregation of the faithful in Pergamos to be reminded of this, because the world is approaching its end and the day of reckoning is at hand. The church in Thyatira is in trouble because it has allowed Jezebel, "which calleth herself a prophetess, to teach and seduce my servants to commit fornication, and to eat things sacrificed unto idols." In case the congregation should be in any doubt as to the seriousness of this, Christ tells them what he is going to do – "I will kill her with death". No one is too inconsequential to be called to account – "all the churches shall know that I am he which searcheth the reins and hearts: and I will give unto every one of you according to your works."

When Christ has done with the seven churches a door opens in heaven and things start to get very strange. A voice, "as it were of a trumpet", tells John that he is about to have revealed to him "things which must be hereafter", and a throne appears with "one", presumably Christ, sitting on it. It is made of costly stones and has a rainbow over it "like unto an emerald". Twenty-four elders with golden crowns sit around the throne from which emerge "lightnings and thunderings and voices" while seven lamps which are the "seven spirits of God" burn before it. There is also a sea of glass and four beasts "full of eyes before and behind". These are like a lion, a calf and an eagle, while one has a "face as a man". They have six pairs of wings each and are "full of eyes within"; they "rest not day and night, saying, Holy, holy, holy, Lord God Almighty; which was, and is, and is to come."

Then John sees a book sealed with seven seals which no one is worthy to open. John weeps at this but is comforted by one of the elders who tells him that "the Lion of the tribe of Juda, the Root of David" is able to break the seals and open the book. After which Christ appears in the form of a slaughtered Lamb "having seven horns and seven eyes, which are the seven Spirits of God sent forth into all the earth." The Lamb takes the book, while the four beasts and the elders and a huge congregation of angels – "ten thousand times ten thousand, and thousands of thousands" – shout "Worthy is the Lamb that was slain to receive power, and riches, and wisdom, and strength, and honour, and glory, and blessing."

There follows the breaking of the seals and the release of the Four Horsemen – the one scene in The Book of Revelation which everyone knows because it has become iconic in European culture through the work of artists as diverse as Albrecht Dürer and Ingmar Bergman.

Not the least of the horsemen is Death who rides out on a pale horse, closely followed by Hell:

> And power was given unto them over the fourth part of the earth, to kill with the sword, and with hunger, and with death, and with the beasts of the earth.

At the breaking of the fifth seal, the souls of those who have been killed for their faith appear. They reveal a lust for revenge which (in the context of the Book of Revelation) does them credit, shouting "with a loud voice",

> How long, O Lord, holy and true, dost thou not judge and avenge our blood on them that dwell on earth?

The souls are given white robes and told to be patient. Their robes have been washed in the blood of the Lamb and their time will come.

Blood plays a big part in The Book of Revelation as it does in the Judaeo-Christian tradition generally, for if you are not washed in the blood of the Lamb, you can be sure you will be soaked in your own, as God takes his revenge. Like George W. Bush, you are either with him or against him.

After the opening of the seventh seal, there is a pause for prayer, then God's ministers, the angels, get down to business. Each of seven angels blows his trumpet, at which "hail and fire mingled with blood" rain down on Earth; a volcano destroys a third of all sea life and shipping; a great star, Wormwood, falls and destroys a third of the Earth's fresh water; a third of the sun, the moon and the stars is also destroyed so that there is a third less daylight. And all this after only four of the angels have blown their trumpets. More and worse is to come, as an angel "flying through the midst of heaven" proclaims, in an advertising break:

> Woe, woe, woe, to the inhabiters of the earth by reason of
> the other voices of the trumpet of the three angels, which
> are yet to sound!

At the next trumpet call, "the bottomless pit" is opened,
spewing out smoke which darkens the sky, as well as locusts and
scorpions with instructions

> that they should not hurt the grass of the earth, neither any
> green thing, neither any tree; but only those men which
> have not the seal of God in their foreheads.

Since the Earth has already been laid waste by storms of hail, fire
and blood, by volcanic eruptions in the sea, a star-fall and the
poisoning of a third of all freshwater, it is a question as to how
many unbelievers are left. But The Book of Revelation is not
about logic, it is about revenge, something which God is very
good at and which he exacts with the skill of a master-torturer.
His instruments, the locusts and scorpions, are instructed

> that they should not kill them [the humans], but that they
> should be tormented five months: and their torment was as
> the torment of a scorpion, when he striketh a man.
> And in those days shall men seek death, and shall not
> find it; and shall desire to die, and death shall flee from
> them.

The reader may be wondering how scorpions and locusts are
to get this done, but these are no ordinary arachnids or insects.
The locusts are like war horses but with the faces of men; they
have women's hair and lions' teeth; breastplates of iron; "and the
sound of their wings *was* as the sound of chariots of many horses
running to battle". They have tails like scorpions, too, and their
sting lasts five months. John omits to describe the scorpions, but
it hardly matters – we get the message.

At the sounding of the sixth trumpet, when an army on horse-
back numbering "two hundred thousand thousand" is let loose to
kill a third of the remaining humans – naturally this force is as
grotesque as the locusts; the cavalrymen have breastplates "of

fire, and of jacinth, and brimstone"; the horses have the heads of lions – the reader may well feel justified in a little catastrophe fatigue. Not so God, who is just warming to the task.

Another angel appears and declares the end of time; John is given a little book to eat; he is told to measure the temple of God, though not the courtyard which is reserved for the Gentiles; two witnesses, the angel says, will testify for "a thousand two hundred *and* threescore days" and anyone who harms them will be killed by fire from their mouths. Eventually, though, the beast in the bottomless pit will emerge and kill the witnesses whose bodies will lie in Sodom for three and a half days before they are resurrected and taken up to heaven. This is bad news for the citizens of Sodom, many of whom are killed in an ensuing earthquake.

But now the seventh angel sounds his trumpet; the time of judgement is at hand, and the temple of God opens to reveal the ark amid "lightnings, and voices, and thunderings, and an earth-quake, and great hail." Events move fast. A mysterious woman, with the sun and the moon at her feet and a crown of stars, gives birth to a son; a red dragon appears which is Satan "which deceiveth the whole world"; there is confusion and war; another dragon appears out of the sea "having seven heads and ten horns, and upon his horns ten crowns, and upon his heads the name of blasphemy". Wonder follows wonder, sign follows sign; there is much destruction and, of course, much blood – when the grapes of the Earth are harvested, "blood came out of the winepress, even unto the horse bridles, by the space of a thousand *and* six hundred furlongs"; the second of the seven plagues is a vial poured by an angel into the sea, "and it became as the blood of a dead *man*: and every living soul died in the sea"; a vial is poured on rivers and fountains "and they became blood".

Men on Earth are burned, suffer sores, are buffeted by huge hailstones, experience terrifying darkness, gnaw their tongues "for pain", all accompanied by the now obligatory lightnings and thunderings and voices and earthquakes, until it is time for the Whore of Babylon to make an appearance, with a banner headline from *The Daily Mail* blazoned on her forehead: "MYSTERY, BABYLON THE GREAT, THE MOTHER OF HARLOTS AND ABOMINATIONS OF THE EARTH". An angel tells John that there is going to be another war against all those who have "fornicated" with her; though by now the reader may well be asking himself why, since the outcome is a foregone conclusion. The final battle nonetheless takes place and all who have sinned are killed, while Satan is bound for a thousand years with "a seal set upon him, that he should deceive the nations no more, till the thousand years should be fulfilled" – though at this point it is hard to imagine who is left on Earth to be deceived.

Meanwhile, the righteous gather round God's throne saying:

> ...Alleluia; Salvation, and glory, and honour, and power, unto the Lord our God:
> For true and righteous are his judgments: for he hath judged the great whore, which did corrupt the earth with her fornication, and hath avenged the blood of his servants at her hand.

A thousand years fly by (even though time is supposed to have ended); the sea gives up its dead, as does hell and death itself; the books are opened for a final settling of accounts, "And whosoever was not found written in the book of life was cast into the lake of fire."

The last two chapters are a winding down. One of the seven angels takes John and shows him the new Jerusalem where "the nations of them which are saved" walk about in the radiance of the Lamb; but, as at the end of a Shakespeare tragedy, there is more a sense of exhaustion and anticlimax, than triumph. Something of the old fieriness and tetchiness of Christ resurfaces at the very end, though, when he threatens that "If any man shall add unto these things, God shall add unto him the plagues that are written in this book",

> And if any man shall take away from the words of the book of this prophecy, God shall take away his part out of the book of life, and out of the holy city, and from the things which are written in this book.

You have been warned.

★

What are we to make of The Revelation of St John? In Christian tradition, it represents the final downward thrust of the great arch of world history that spans from the Creation in Genesis. When it says THE END in capitals on the last page of the Authorised Version, it means it. Many fundamentalists still take The Book of Revelation seriously, glossing the prophecy, and seeking parallels and signs in our own age, just as Christians have done for centuries – for the end time is always just around the corner. Such belief can have serious implications. It has had a subliminal influence on American policy toward Israel, for example, since many fundamentalists believe that the founding of the Israeli state and the return of all Jews are necessary prerequisites to Armageddon and the Rapture.

But if you do not take The Revelation at face value, you have to ask questions. It is tempting to interpret it as the work of someone under the influence of hallucinatory drugs; or it may be a schizophrenic; or the description of a nightmare. Yet what strikes me most is the way in which its imagery is typical of a second-rate imagination. All those monsters with multiple heads and crowns; all that blood; all the thunder and lightning; the hail and earthquakes; all those trumpets and stentorian voices – this is the world of Marvel Comics or Hammer Films. It is good fun, but hardly to be taken as a reliable guide to the future of the universe.

Despite this, millions of Christians *have* taken it as such a guide, and millions do so today. This says something about the status of religion in human affairs. During the past two hundred years, science has produced a mass of evidence about the nature of the material universe which has systematically refuted the comic-book world of The Revelation, so much so that to persist in taking it seriously is akin to a self-willed hallucinatory madness. To the extent that all religions have this element in them, religion itself may be considered a form of self-validating group psychosis. In our society if you have hallucinations that are unique to yourself you are said to be insane and will be given psychiatric treatment whether you agree to it or not. But if enough people believe in what is self-evidently a hallucination, then it is all right; you are not mad, you have seen the light.

As material conditions worsen this century, we may well see a resurgence of fundamentalist Christianity in the affluent West. Were it to become a dominant force, socially and politically, establishing a consensus of dogmatic belief, then it may be that rationalists and atheists will come to be viewed as insane, for they will have rejected "truths" which are self-evident to believers, even though no evidence will, or can, be adduced in their defence. If society remains comparatively humane (though this is by no means certain, as events since 11 September, 2001 have suggested), atheists may perhaps be sectioned for their own good, and treated with drugs and other therapies until they are "cured". Then we would be in a world that is at least as mad as the one that erupted from the head of St John the Divine.

THE INCOMPLETENESS OF BEING HUMAN

If you know the lives of almost any family, you will know that behind the exterior which they present to the world there is a tangled mass of dissatisfactions and longings, inadequacies real or imagined, a frustrated sense of fulfilment postponed or blocked. The grass is always greener on the other side of the fence, we say, to persuade each other that we should be satisfied with our lot. It is good advice; but there is still that fence and the promise of greener conditions beyond it; and "lot" is too close to "allotted", to the suggestion that we have little or no control over the circumstances of our lives. Even if we have such control, or a modicum of it, we make mistakes, choose the wrong husband or wife; the wrong career; we grind away at the daily routine; are depressed for no apparent reason; are overtaken by illness or the sudden death of those close to us. We devise ways to escape all this, through the oblivion of drink or drugs, holidays that take us to ever more distant and exotic locations where life could be different – it's paradise there, we say; we even relocate to the south of France or Spain hoping that somehow this will heal the wound of being human. We block our ears and fill our heads with music from iPods and Walkmen; yet when the playlist is exhausted, our sense of incompleteness returns. Deep down, it was Wordsworth's "still, sad music of humanity" that we listened to all the time.

With the possible exception of our closest living relatives, the chimpanzees, only humans appear to be like this. It is impossible to know what Gerard Manley Hopkins would call the inscape of a chaffinch or a swift, of course, but observing them it is difficult not to feel that they are complete. They can suffer from disease or accident, their nests can be predated or their habitat destroyed, yet in themselves, in their brief existence in time, a chaffinch or a swift has an integrity that cannot be improved on. A swift is a swift is a swift, and you can only follow its rapid, flickering flight and piercing screams with admiration.

In this, birds leave humans far behind, because even though many species are capable of learned behaviour, their nature is essentially instinctive. In birds, being and action are one. Humans also have many traits that are instinctive – more, perhaps, than we like to admit to – but because of the way in which the brain evolved in the genus *Homo*, with a steady increase in size in relation to body weight over a period of two million years, we have become, in *Homo sapiens*, a species that can think, that can plan ahead, and above all in this context, can conceptualise alternative existences.

While the two species of chimpanzees may have these traits in embryonic form, humans have them to a degree that is unique. They are what powered the cultural explosion in East Africa 50,000 years ago and what gave us the concept of progress, driving the speeded-up nature of technological change in our own era. But they are also at the root of our inherent sense of incompleteness, of our dissatisfaction with the present, because we can imagine it being different.

This is why consumer capitalism has been so successful. Order this fitted kitchen, buy this car, take this luxury cruise and you will be fulfilled, is the subtext of the advertisements and the colour supplements, the showrooms and on-line catalogues. And because the accumulation of possessions only achieves this momentarily, the system lures us on. We upgrade to a four-wheel drive even though we live in a suburb; add on a conservatory even though we don't know what to do with it; take ever more exotic holidays, ending in the icy wastes of Antarctica or the coral beaches of Micronesia. Consumerism can never complete us, nor is that its intention, because it depends on our sense of being incomplete and the allure of desire.

Incompleteness is also at the heart of religion. "Man that is born of woman hath but a short time to live, and is full of misery. He cometh up, and is cut down, like a flower; he fleeth as it were a shadow, and never continueth in one stay," intones the priest in The Burial of the Dead. Incompleteness, Christians believe, is inherent in the conditions of life on Earth. Not here, not now, but across the great divide created by death is where completion may be found. "Thou knowest, Lord, the secrets of our hearts; shut not thy merciful ears to our prayer; but spare us, Lord most holy, O God most mighty, O holy and merciful Saviour, thou most worthy Judge eternal, suffer us not, at our last hour, for any pains of death, to fall from thee."

Only through union with God after death, when the veil is torn away, can completion be attained. That is why death is so momentous, why the priest at the graveside intones the many names of God to placate him; for the righteous are completed but the sinful are judged and cast into Hell, their incompleteness perpetuated into a dark eternity. This is still a basic Christian belief across the world, *pace* liberal Christians who have abandoned the concept of Hell.

Buddhism, if it can be called a religion, seeks completeness by rubbing away at the stone of desire until nothing is left and the individual is released into no-desire, the completion of a kind of unbeing on Earth and the prospect of oblivion in death. Stoicism, too, distances itself from desire, seeking completeness in a standing back from the world in scorn at what it can offer.

Most religions are collective affairs. There is a community of worshippers and a priesthood that acts as the god's intermediary on Earth. The sense of human incompleteness is individual but it is also shared. There is another branch of activity, however, which engages with the nature of being human, and that is literature, which, though its *raison d'être* is the sharing of experience with readers, is the product of the unique imagination of individual minds. Poetry and fiction are particularly fascinating in the context of this discussion because at their heart is a paradox: that many of the greatest poems and novels are predicated on, and explore, the wound of human incompleteness, yet are aesthetically complete in themselves. It is this which makes them so engaging and at the same time so disturbing to read, whether it is

Shakespeare's *Hamlet*, Conrad's *Lord Jim*, or Eliot's *The Waste Land*.

There is a further paradox in that one of the deepest motivations of the writer is the search for personal completeness through the act of creation. "No one can leap over his shadow," Coleridge wrote; "poets leap over Death." Any reader knows what he means. Coleridge's poems, the *Biographia Literaria*, the Notebooks, give collectively the aura of the man. To have read Coleridge is to know him in the deepest possible way; to know that part of the creative mind which did indeed leap over death to achieve a posthumous existence in the minds of future generations.

Yet there is an irony here, for the completeness of the imaginative act is almost always achieved at the expense of the writer's personal life which, as in Coleridge's case, can be spectacularly incomplete. Moreover, the damage the writer inflicts on himself spreads outwards. The lives of Coleridge and his younger contemporaries Shelley and Byron, to take just three examples from the Romantic period, are littered with the hurt and sometimes terrible harm they inflicted on those who thought it possible to love them.

For the writer is single-minded. Whatever else he may be obliged to do, his inner life circles the creative act as if it were a camp fire on a vast plain. When writing he is most alive, yet as a person he is almost a cipher. When the work is finished, he re-enters his old familiar self with all its unfinished business, becomes incomplete again.

In his way, the poet or novelist imitates a creator god; he breathes life into something that has never existed before; creates perfection out of the imperfection of being human. But he must do it again and again, seeking the momentary completion of the imaginative act. That is why meeting authors is usually a disappointment. We are drawn to them through their work; what attracts is the intensity of the inner life on display in the poem or novel. In person, though, when they step down from the mountain, they can seem as ordinary as ourselves; worried about the guttering, obsessed with their health. So we come away wondering why we wanted to know them at all.

Humans will never be complete, though we will never cease to dream of it. For the time being it is genetic engineering and nanotechnology that we set our sights on. No more birth defects or inherited diseases; no more manic depression or schizophrenia; a world of smiling people as in the pastel illustrations to the Jehovah's Witnesses' magazines. There will be progress but it will not bring completeness because our thinking brains tripped a switch 50,000 years ago that we cannot turn off. "*Quando fiam uti chelidon*", When will I be like the swallow? laments the voice in *The Waste Land*. We cannot return to the pure being of the birds. Instead we have art to express the incompleteness of what we are in a perfect aesthetic form; and we have, and no doubt always will have, the dubious consolations of religion.

JUDAS

For two thousand years Judas has been vilified as the man who betrayed Jesus. Yet I can't help feeling that this is undeserved. The assumption is that he *chose* to betray the Saviour of Mankind and that therefore his place in Hell is assured. Free will, however, is a problem Christians skate over as often as they can.

How free, for example, was Judas, or any of the disciples, or Jesus himself? Biblical exegetes have been adept for two millennia at finding passages in the Old Testament that prophesy incidents in the life of Christ. They are still at it, as five minutes on the doorstep with a Jehovah's Witness will confirm. If we suppose for the moment that the exegetes are right, then the whole of Jesus's life was mapped out from the start.

It could be argued, of course, that as God Incarnate, Jesus is an exception and the question of free will or otherwise does not apply. It might still be possible, therefore, to make a case for the operation of free will on the part of Judas. When, at the Last Supper, Jesus says "Verily, I say unto you, One of you which eateth with me shall betray me", he is careful not to name the traitor. Murmurs of "Is it I?" go round the table, but Jesus is evasive: "*It is* one of the twelve, that dippeth with me in the dish." There is an obvious escape route for free will here, though, as the Son of God, it is doubtful that Jesus did not know which of the disciples it was.

Shortly afterwards Jesus makes another prophecy, telling Peter, specifically this time: "Verily I say unto thee, That this day, *even* in this night, before the cock crow twice, thou shalt deny me thrice."

More than once in the Gospels it is clear that Jesus has foreseen everything, including his own crucifixion. How could it be otherwise if he is God Incarnate? It is reasonable to ask, therefore, what scope Peter had to exercise free will when the Last Supper was over and the disciples got up from the table? If in that fateful dawn he had not denied Jesus, then the prophecy would have been wrong, and in biblical terms that is an impossibility. Peter *had* to denounce Jesus and he moved toward the crowing of the cock as if in a dream. As Jesus says later in the Garden of Gethsemane, "the scriptures must be fulfilled".

The disjunction between free will and predestination is, in fact, a head-on collision between irreconcilables that tears apart the fabric of the Bible. The books of the Old and New Testaments form a great span of world history from the Creation in Genesis to the destruction of the material universe in The Book of Revelation. In between, character after character, event after event, presages what is to come, with the birth, works, and crucifixion of Jesus at the centre. Prophecy is not guesswork, sometimes hitting the mark and sometimes shooting wide of it. The Bible is the word of God and the prophets are his mouthpiece. Everything that is prophesied has to happen; there is no room for the either/or of free will. If you believe, that is.

Outside the hot house of biblical exegesis, things look different. There, free will is a messy concept, hedged in by constraints, only some of which may be known. We say we have free will, and its putative existence is fundamental to our social transactions. We recognise, though, that an individual's free will can be impaired, especially through mental illness. If someone commits a crime during a period of schizophrenia or paranoia, his mental condition can be used in evidence; he was, the defence can argue, "not responsible for his actions". This may be why so many of us draw back from the mentally ill; their ability to choose freely is whirled away with their delusions; they challenge our assumptions about the steady-state of the mind and our personality.

Even without mental illness, however, our freedom to choose has to be questioned. There is what must be a universal constraint in that we are made out of elements that are found throughout the universe. This may be a weak constraint that can be ignored for practical purposes. But the evolutionary direction of the molecules and their constituent atoms that form our bodies cannot be dismissed so easily. Leaving aside the first 3.5 billion years of life on Earth, we are a product of the Cambrian "explosion" of 530 million years ago, when multicellular life burgeoned and diversified at an extraordinary rate. Among the Cambrian fossils of the Burgess shale in Canada is to be found a chordate, the earliest known example of the phylum that led through numerous pathways to the mammals, and eventually through bushy clades of apes and early hominids, to us.

Many aspects of these evolutionary twists and turns affect what we are – the ratio between body mass and the size of our brains, for example, bipedalism, opposable thumbs. The substrate of our behaviour is conditioned by our evolutionary development. We are a highly refined species of great ape and, as such, social animals governed by the obligations of kinship and the mutual self-interest of social networks. The latter become weaker with distance, however; a fact which makes it extremely difficult for politicians to pursue idealistic social policies in which the individual is asked to make sacrifices (through increased taxation, for example) in the name of the greater good of the many. It is much easier to appeal to the individual's self-interest – as we have seen during the past thirty years – by cutting taxation so that the individual *feels* better off, even though this means declining standards in areas such as health, the social services, education, and transport that affect everyone except the very rich.

Our nature as social animals means that we are very susceptible to mass suggestion; we follow fashion rather than making up our own minds, because we do not want to isolate ourselves by appearing different. Even when we rebel against society at large by becoming a skinhead or a punk, we are conforming to the ethos of a group. True dissidents, though they exist, are very rare.

Under these conditions, where is there room for free will? Many traditional societies actively discourage it; conformity is the norm, and deviation is punished by ostracism or worse. Mass society, with its atomised economic individuals, may seem more congenial to the operation of free will of sorts. In practice, however, this is often reduced to, and confused with, "consumer choice", where fashion and advertising act as powerful conforming influences on inherently selfish behaviour.

Free will in the biblical sense – that is, the individual's ability to choose between good and evil – must by definition be governed by the same constraints. When an individual finds a wallet in the street and takes it to the police station, while another silently pockets it, it is easy to say that the one has made an honest decision, and the other a dishonest one. But how far free will had a hand in this is another matter. It is quite possible that genetically inherited traits over which they had no effective control, influenced the behaviour of both individuals. Certainly nurture is likely to have played a part – how each was brought up at home and at school, for example. Yet it is almost impossible to quantify with certainty the contribution of any of these factors to the decision to return the wallet or to steal it. Seeing the wallet lying in the road, we say we have a choice, but that choice may have been made for us in all essentials, thousands or even millions of years ago.

When we come to the problem of Judas, the shadow of predestination has also to be considered, as it falls across the Bible, and across the men and women who act out their parts under the watchful eye of the God of Wrath. For in biblical terms, Jesus *had* to be crucified if he was to fulfil his destiny as the Saviour of Mankind. And one of the disciples *had* to betray him – "the scriptures must be fulfilled". Judas, like Peter, was playing a role in a great drama that was scripted long before.

Given this, why should he be condemned, as he has been over the centuries? Should he not, instead, be considered for canonization by the Roman Catholic Church? It would be late in the day, but better late than never, and it would redress an injustice – the double bind which made it impossible for Judas to act in any other way, sacrificed, as he had to be, on the altar of Jesus' divine mission. This has no doubt occurred to others in the past and will have been refuted by theologians – to their satisfaction, at least. To a non-believer, though, the fact remains: according to the inner logic of the Bible and the unfolding of God's plan for the universe as revealed there, Judas had no choice; there was no free will.

THE APE IN US

When Linnaeus came to classify humans in his pioneering taxonomy of all living things, he gave us our own genus, *Homo*, adding the species indicator, *sapiens*. At the time, humans appeared to be unique. Today the genus *Homo* is populated with at least half a dozen other related species of hominid. It is a question, though, whether we should have a separate genus, or whether in strict taxonomic terms we should share a genus with the chimpanzees, for recent studies have revealed the remarkable genetic affinity that exists between humans and the most intelligent of the great apes.

Genetics have transformed taxonomy with the result that many other species have been assigned to quite different genera from the ones they were given using traditional criteria. We are unlikely to reclassify ourselves, however. We know that historically we are one among several human species that have roamed the world, we cling, nonetheless, to the notion of human exceptionalism, and to merge the genera *Pan* and *Homo* would involve a revolution in the way we think about ourselves.

Nonetheless the relationship between humans and chimpanzees continues to worry us. Medical researchers and other scientists have long valued chimpanzees as experimental subjects. Experiments on chimpanzees can and have been justified on the grounds that they are animals, and that experiments on them can lead to advances in medicine which will be of great benefit to humankind. It is precisely because of its proximity to humanity that *Pan troglodytes* is so valuable. If the relationship had been more distant, the chimpanzee would be less suitable as a subject.

So long as it can be kept on the right side of the animal-human divide, things can be done to chimpanzees that would constitute cruel and unnatural practice if applied to humans.

But that convenient divide keeps breaking down, for it is impossible for most people to watch film footage of chimpanzees in laboratories and not see in them a reflection of ourselves. It would be interesting to know what psychological damage has been inflicted on researchers, acknowledged or unacknowledged, over the many years of experimentation on apes. Recognition of this seepage across the boundary between chimpanzees and humans eventually led to one of the most successful campaigns against animal experimentation. Most chimpanzee laboratories, so far as I am aware, have been closed down. The experimenters have reluctantly moved on to species of monkeys.

Even if we come to recognise more fully our close kinship, however, it is unlikely to change the fate of the great apes – the orang-utan, the mountain gorilla and the two species of chimpanzee. It is estimated that all will become extinct in the wild within a few decades due to deforestation, hunting, and war. They will survive in the world's great zoos, though, behind bars and behind glass, and then we will have to face their eyes.

For the eyes of the great apes are their most disturbing feature. Many aspects of their physical presence – hirsuteness, knuckle-walking – mark them off from us as "animals", but you cannot look into the eyes of a chimpanzee or a gorilla and fail to be moved. Moist, brown, they look deeply into our eyes, as if sight could speak; as if the barrier created by human possession of language and the lack of it on their part is irrelevant for the moment. It is impossible to feel this about the eyes of cats that open and close like Asiatic curtains; or the black pillar-box slots of the eyes of goats and sheep.

The eyes of the great apes are human eyes, or so close, that in the end you have to turn away from their gaze, which seems not accusatory but thoughtful, as if weighing us up, undecided as yet. It is a relief to emerge from the ape house into the sunlight and the screaming and stalking and restless activity of the other animals, though you know you have left something of yourself behind in the foetor of the tropically-heated cages.

This perception of the humanness of the apes must be very ancient. Orang-utan, from the Malay *orang-utan*, means "forest man"; gorilla is said to be "African" for "wild man" in a Greek account of a voyage of the fifth or sixth century BC. Glimpsing an orang-utan squatting in a rainforest canopy, or a gorilla moving slowly across a forested slope, it is easy to see why they were conflated with some form of unknown human, existing at the edge of our world and our consciousness.

Press photographs in 2008 showed a group of dead gorillas discovered in the Congo, bound on stretchers made from poles lashed together, their heads thrown back, their huge barrel chests thrust up against the sky. They had presumably been hunted and killed for "bush meat" and the hunters disturbed as they were about to carry them off.

The scene was like a grotesque re-enactment of the crucifixion of Christ and the two thieves. Christians believe this to have been the central moment in the history of humanity, when God's mercy streamed down on us through his suffering Son. The photographs showed the deposition; the suffering of the gorillas was over.

There was nothing redeeming in the image, however, though there was much that was troubling – the way in which the gorillas seemed so reminiscent of humans; the way in which their deaths at human hands echoed the deaths of tens of millions of humans killed by our own species in the twentieth century.

We will never be able to kill all life on Earth, no matter how hard we try, but in the destructive rampage we are embarked on, we can and will destroy a vast array of species currently alive. There could be no more fitting memorial to humans, when we too fall victim to extinction, than the bronze statues of three crucified gorillas, set on a tropical hill. Birds would alight on them at times; below in the recovering forest, seething, bustling, snapping life would reconfigure itself, over the millions of years that are yet to come.

JUNK CULTURE

During the past decade there has been a sporadic and inconclusive debate about the "dumbing down" of culture. There are those who are convinced that this is taking place. Others argue that what we are seeing is a movement away from elitist ideas of culture as the preserve of the educated middle class to a people's culture which, spread laterally, is more inclusive and more in keeping with twenty-first century society and its needs. There is a third possibility, that both high culture and popular culture are being challenged by a new phenomenon, junk culture, a form of hybridisation unique to the atomised world we now inhabit, where relationships are increasingly mediated electronically via the internet, the mobile phone, television and radio.

A major consequence of this, through the proliferation of blogs, personal websites and chat rooms, has been the pseudo-democratisation of critical opinion whereby anyone can have his or her say on any subject in a more or less public forum, and where every opinion is said to be equally valid.

This trend has spread outwards in various ways. Amazon encourages readers to post their own reviews of books and give them a starred assessment which then become part of the promotional package as you browse the site. Newspapers offer "Have your say" options on their websites where readers can comment on the day's news. This is different from a conventional Letters Column where only a fraction of letters submitted ever gets published and where editorial selection weeds out absurd or abusive submissions. Television and radio stations have similar options, even posting selected comments from viewers during broadcasts from time to time. A number of these sites operate with some form of screening process but others do not.

At the time of the millennium celebrations there was a good deal of retrospective comment on the achievements of the twentieth century. Frequently, even in the serious press, this took the form of lists of The Twenty Best Films, The Twenty Best Novels and so on, based on readers' votes. It was clear from these lists that most readers who responded had a limited knowledge of film or literature in the twentieth century. Silent films were almost entirely absent, as was film noir, and Italian and French cinema from the great decades of the 1950s and 60s. Only a few European films at all, such as Ingmar Bergman's *The Seventh Seal*, made it through. Instead, the lists were weighted toward films or books published in the last twenty years during the lifetime of the voters. It would have been much more informative to have invited leading critics to contribute essays on the subject, but this was rarely done.

The drive toward opinion has affected newspapers in another way. Hard news coverage is steadily being marginalised and replaced by columnists who offer opinion on items in the news. Some columnists are good but they are rarely experts in the fields they comment on. They can only offer an opinion which may be intelligent or may be merely opinionated. Frequently the columnist's e-mail address is included so readers can respond with an opinion on the columnist's opinion.

There is a reductive element in this process which has led to a popular suspicion of expertise as elitist. The considered judgement of an individual who has spent a lifetime reading and thinking about, say, the novel, weighs no more in the balance than that of a casual reader. It is merely one opinion. The only fair way to arrive at a judgement is to collect many opinions through a vote. The novel which receives most votes is the best. Some experts, seduced by postmodernism, have willingly colluded in this, dismissing attempts at informed value judgement as connoisseurial or belletrist.

There is, however, a general confusion over the meanings of *elite*, *elitist*, and *elitism*. To many people they suggest privilege and snobbery based on unearned wealth, social position, or educational advantage. They conjure up a society divided by class prejudice of a kind that is no longer acceptable. We decline to defer to, or be ruled by, our public-school and Oxford- and Cambridge-educated "betters" – or so we like to think. (New Labour and Conservative cabinets of the past thirty years have, nonetheless, been dominated by Oxford and Cambridge graduates, with many Conservative ministers having public school backgrounds as well.)

Because of this, *elitist* and *elitism* have negative connotations attached to them of a kind which means that they can only be used pejoratively. There is a case, though, for retaining *elite* as a neutral term to describe what actually goes on in society, because any complex society depends on a criss-crossing of elites – in the sense of specialists – for it to operate. If I have to undergo open heart surgery, I want a consultant who is highly trained in that complex area of surgery, not someone armed with Grey's *Anatomy* and a scalpel; the same is true if I want a house built; or if I want to know the latest thinking in the field of palaeoanthropology. Many individuals in society are specialists in this way and form, in a purely descriptive sense, elites.

It is when we come to the arts that problems arise. Only a small number of people at any one time are capable of mastering the knowledge and surgical techniques needed to become a heart surgeon. Most people can write, however, and junk culture encourages the assumptive leap that most people can become writers if they want to. There have always been amateur writers, as there have been amateur painters. In the eighteenth and nineteenth centuries, turning out a passable sonnet or watercolour was considered a necessary accomplishment among men and women of the gentry. This was recognised, however, for what it was – a pleasant pursuit which gave the individual a form of artistic expression, but which was not to be confused with the work of professional writers and painters.

Many people still write and paint in this way, but junk culture has blurred the distinctions by claiming to professionalise the amateur. This is especially noticeable in literature as a result of the rapid spread of "creative writing" programmes in universities. Every campus now has such a programme, usually as an offshoot of the English department, though in some cases as a department in its own right. As a result, students can practise writing instead of merely reading it, and can progress, if they wish, to a creative writing MA and even a creative writing PhD.

At one level attempting to write, say, free verse while studying the great twentieth-century exponents of it can be instructive. "No verse is free for the man who wants to do a good job," as T.S. Eliot observed. Experimenting with free verse yourself is a good way of finding this out, discovering in the process something of the subtlety and difficulty of the form, which in turn feeds back into your reading.

The lure of creative writing programmes, though, is that they purport to offer something else – not an enhanced understanding of what you read, but the chance to train to become a writer yourself, and not an amateur in the old sense either, but a professional with letters after your name to prove it. This pseudo-professionalization leads to the expectation that your work will be published, and creative writing departments encourage this, many of them producing annual anthologies of MA students' work which, thanks to advances in desktop publishing, look wholly professional, even though they are in fact a form of private publication. The better students are also encouraged to submit to literary magazines, with covering letters often indicating that Dr —— recommended them to do so. In my experience such work is rarely more than competent and little different from hundreds of other submissions a literary editor receives. When faced year after year with piles of mediocre course work in the form of stories and poems it is understandable that creative writing tutors are tempted to exaggerate to themselves the quality of work that is marginally better, and that they encourage in this way the students who produced it.

Every literary editor will have had the experience of being bombarded with submissions from an eager young poet or fiction writer only for him or her to disappear without trace after a few years. The would-be author has given up and moved on. With increasing frequency such aspirants are drawn from the ranks of creative writing graduates. It would be pleasant to report that after abandoning a literary career themselves they turned to creative reading, subscribing to the literary magazines, buying the latest poetry and fiction titles from publishers like Seren or Gomer – becoming, in other words, part of the class of intelligent readers who have been the backbone of literary culture since the early eighteenth century. That this is not the case is proved by the continuing low sales figures for most poetry and new fiction titles, and by the low circulation figures of the literary magazines. (Many of the latter have even declined in recent years.) Instead, we live in a culture where paradoxically there are far more poets than there are readers of poetry who, if they were a species, would be put on the Red List.

This trend feeds into junk culture and is probably not unrelated to the absence of poetry and the decline of serious reviewing in the daily press. Newspapers as diverse as *The Independent* and *The Daily Telegraph* have relegated literary reviews to the back pages of Friday or Saturday cultural supplements where they tend to be few in number and short. Up front and given prominence with large-format colour photographs are artist profiles which concentrate on a writer's or a pop musician's personality, "life-style" and so on. In this way literature, music and art are subsumed in the glossy, materialist, feel-good ethos that has spread throughout the serious dailies, especially after most of them changed to a tabloid format.

Even the political pages are not exempt. When Nicholas Sarkozy, the President of France, made a state visit to England in 2008, as much attention was paid to the looks and deportment of his new wife, Carla Bruni, as to Sarkozy himself and the serious politics that the visit included. "Did Carla Do it for You?" was a front-page sideline in *The Independent* for 29 March, pointing readers in the direction of a double-page spread, the left-hand page of which was a head-and-shoulders colour portrait of the ex-model, while the right offered differing opinions by two women columnists and yet more photographs. The paper's third leader was also devoted favourably to Carla Bruni, while yet another columnist, Bonnie Greer, provided what might be called balance with her enthusiastic endorsement of Sarkozy himself as a hunk: "He was a walking energy field. One hundred per cent testosterone, the way that Russell Crowe is," she gushed. There was one serious report on the economic problems facing Sarkozy on his return to France.

Carla Bruni Sarkozy is a beautiful woman. Had she not been, she would have been ignored by the press, no matter how well she deported herself. Like Princess Diana before her, she has what the tabloids and now even the serious press demand – beauty and sexiness in close proximity to power. This has always been an intoxicating combination – think of Helen of Troy, Queen Guinevere – but in the past, limited means of communication meant that such figures were remote from the people and experienced in transfigured form through heroic poetry and romance. The pervasiveness of print and especially electronic media in our lives has changed this. Were Helen alive today, she would be the subject not of poets but the paparazzi and there would be telephoto images of her in *The Sun* sunbathing topless on a luxury yacht off the Turkish coast.

In the contemporary world, fact and fiction have become hopelessly scrambled, thanks to the media. The idealising tendency of the Hollywood film industry and American television, combined with the ubiquity of colour photography, mean that we are constantly presented with images of beautiful women and handsome men as if they were the norm. From *Sex and the City* to *Friends* to the readers of the news, you will rarely see anyone who is ugly or old. Beauty made manifest as sexual attraction is also a staple of the advertising industry, for as advertising agencies have discovered, sex can be used to sell anything from cars to cereals. Beauty-as-sex also sells magazines – there is hardly a glossy on the racks at a newsagent's that doesn't have a sexually attractive woman or a macho male on its cover.

It is unsurprising that the arts have also been drawn into this vortex of sexualisation. Sex has always played a part in pop music, but now it is influencing the presentation of classical music, at least on its fringes, with singers such as Kathryn Jenkins being presented as Hollywood starlets, as much in demand for their bodies as their voices; likewise the attractive Japanese virtuoso who allowed herself to be photographed in a wet T-shirt on the beach with her violin. In magazines like *The American Poetry Review*, judging from publicity shots, every other female poet has just come off the set of *Sex and the City*. Most poets, though, still look reassuringly mundane in photographs on dust jackets. It is a question as to whether this is not a factor in the unpopularity of the genre.

The sexualisation of our culture is so prevalent that we have come to think of it as the norm. In many parts of the world, however, this is still not the case. On visits to cities like Istanbul, and Georgetown, Guyana, I have been momentarily surprised by the absence of sexual images on public display; then relieved at not having to face what amounts to corporate soft pornography with its fascistic idealisation at every step. Its absence leaves you space to inhabit your own skin and to respond freely to the reality of the world. In Georgetown and Istanbul there were many beautiful young women who had a natural grace that is now very rare in Britain.

Those whom the gods love die young, was the saying. Those whom the people idolise are turned on and brought tumbling down. Junk culture is a vicious culture. Beautiful women, especially those who have little apart from their beauty, are vulnerable to the fickleness of mass adoration which consists in a powerful mix of sentimentality, envy and anger. Sexualised beauty is raised up, pursued, pried into by the media; it sells newspapers because people have become conditioned to needing it in their lives. But it is always beyond their grasp; a fantasy that is belied every time they open their door and walk onto the street. At every turn, commodified culture mocks us with the unattainable by making the ideal sexualised vision of life seem so desirable and so natural. If you're not like this, then what are you, the advertisements, the glossy magazines, the films, the television shows demand.

The disjunction between the ideal and the real creates a deep, repressed anxiety and anger that are only waiting for an excuse to erupt into collective rage. The mob attacks on paedophiles in the 1990s should be seen in this light. Here was a group of men – tabloids like *The News of the World* repeatedly told their readers – who could and should be hunted down. The mobs who gathered outside known paedophiles' homes, shattering their windows; who in one case attacked a paediatrician's office in the belief that anything with "paed" in it must be suspect; who drove a number of convicted paedophiles to suicide and felt self-righteous about it afterwards, were displacing a much more diffuse anger onto a group against whom rage and violence were sanctioned by the tabloids.

Mass rage is closely allied to mass sentimentality. Because of this it can be extremely dangerous to court the media and be adored by the people. The most fascinating example is Princess Diana. Beautiful, wealthy, the consort of the Crown Prince and the future Queen of England, she combined in an uncanny way junk culture's deep obsession with sexualised power. She was also neurotic, unhappy, wounded by a fatally flawed marriage – and adept at manipulating the tabloid press in order to stoke the adulation she desperately craved and to gain revenge on her estranged husband and his family.

She became the "People's Princess", a vulgarised fairy-tale character in haute couture who looked and acted like a Hollywood starlet, yet had "problems" just like the rest of us. The saga of her failing marriage was played out publicly – and deliberately – in the tabloids, and for a long time Charles and his mistress Camilla were the subject of a campaign of vilification in parts of the press. They had to bide their time, for whatever the truth of the matter, they could not compete with the doe-eyed innocence and elegance, and media manipulation, of Diana.

When she was killed, Diana was at the height of her reign over the tabloids and their readers. The outflow of grief – with people who had never met her crying openly in the streets, the sea of flowers in protective cellophane in London, the sense that to demur was to court ostracism or worse – was the biggest expression of public sentimentality in modern times. And it had, as its close companion, a barely suppressed rage. When Buckingham Palace failed to hoist the royal standard at half mast, on the grounds that the Queen was in Scotland and protocol demanded that it could only be raised when she was in residence, the tabloids began to turn on her. In public, Elizabeth II had always remained successfully aloof from Charles and Diana's marital breakdown, retaining the affection of the tabloids in the process. Now the tabloids threatened to drag her into the vortex. Very quickly the Queen retreated, protocol was broken with, and the royal standard appeared on the palace at half mast even though she was not there. The baying *vox populi* had been heard.

Had she lived, Diana's star would have dimmed as her beauty faded; a People's Princess must be young and pretty for ever. She would even have been cast out of tabloid heaven had she married Dodi Al-Fayed; for then she would have lost the charisma of sexualised power that she exercised by virtue of her association with royalty; she would have become another rich man's wife, living on yachts and in expensive hotels, seen at the right restaurants and parties, angling for a spread in *Hello!* or *OK!* magazine. As it turned out, of course, Diana, our modern huntress, was devoured by her own hounds, the paparazzi.

In a remarkably short time, the tears of the people were wiped away, and Diana became more or less forgotten. The Diana Museum on her brother's estate, which was to have been a permanent memorial to her, has been a failure with the public – a display of designer gowns and other memorabilia of the once beautiful dead. Other women have taken her place, though none so far has managed to combine the deep appeal of royalty, sexualised power, and victimhood, which made her the epitome of junk culture. Press hysteria during the visit of Carla Bruni Sarkozy to England in 2008 was an exploratory attempt at finding a replacement. Journalists were right to perceive that some of the elements were there – beauty and poise that upstaged her husband-politician (as the press reported it); a love match (in a reversal of the Charles, Diana, Camilla triangle) that followed on from a very public divorce; but it didn't quite gel. Madame Sarkozy appears at least to be more mature than Diana and she is lucky enough to be foreign and not to live in England.

Junk culture also takes its toll on ordinary people who become exposed to its attention. The disappearance in Portugal of Madeleine McCann, the young daughter of Kate and Gerry McCann, had the right ingredients for an outpouring of sentimentality and outrage that the British tabloids and their readers feed on. The little girl was photogenic in her innocence, Kate McCann beautiful, and her husband handsome, while the Portuguese police, who may have conducted a less than thorough investigation, were available for vituperation – things would have been different, it was implied, had the case been handled by the British police.

The disappearance filled the media for weeks, then months; from the beginning, though, all was not right from the tabloids' point of view. Kate and Gerry McCann made the requisite televised appeals for the abductor to return Madeleine and for anyone with information to come forward. The parents, however, did not behave as was expected of them. Convention dictates that the mother should be tearful, preferably breaking down in front of the cameras. The husband can be stoic and supportive, but it should it be clear that he is holding back his emotions. Evidence of vulnerablity is essential if the pact with the tabloids is to hold. The McCanns were not like this. Intelligent, middle-class professionals, they held in their anguish; Kate McCann did not cry on screen; they were brisk and efficient in the way they dealt with the media, and adept at gaining publicity for their disappeared daughter. They broke the unwritten agreement, refusing to behave as victims on whom junk culture could lavish its sentimentality in return for maximum exposure. The McCanns used the media, instead of the media using them.

That was a dangerous strategy. Junk culture can be merciless through its agents, the tabloids, when anybody who crosses it is perceived to be vulnerable to attack. When Kate and Gerry McCann were formally declared to be "suspects" by the Portuguese police, even though the term does not mean quite what it would under British law, they were paid back. No hard evidence was ever produced to implicate them in the disappearance of their daughter, but for weeks the tabloid press blazoned every rumour, every spurious leak from the police, in banner headlines on their front pages. Having failed to turn them into victims, the tabloids rounded on the McCanns and effectively put them on trial, acting as council for the prosecution, judge and jury, and coming close to finding them guilty.

Such an onslaught would have daunted many people, but Kate and Gerry McCann fought back, demanding and getting through their lawyers a front page apology and damages from *The Daily Express* and *The Daily Star* who were the worst offenders. It appears to be a rare instance of junk culture frustrated and outmanoeuvred. Were evidence to emerge at a later date implicating the McCanns in the disappearance of their daughter – something which is highly improbable and which I don't think will happen – the tabloids would take a savage revenge.

Intelligence is the enemy of junk culture, because it is not easily amenable to control. It can be dismissed, though, through mockery. *Planet* magazine was once referred to in *The Western Mail* as "the magazine for clever people", and in junk culture the last thing you want to appear is clever. What would be considered an intellectual elite in Continental Europe – in the neutral sense of *elite* defined earlier – is frequently dismissed in England as "the chattering classes", suggesting the insignificance of intellectuals; their irrelevance to what goes on in the real world where *doing* is what counts. Significantly, the term has been taken over by many intellectuals as a form of protective camouflage. Self-deprecation and self-mockery are permitted.

Wales is deeply implicated in this trend. When Zaha Hadid's design was selected for a proposed new opera house in Cardiff, *The Western Mail* – "Papur Genedlaethol Cymru" as its masthead proclaims – led a vociferous campaign against it. Zaha Hadid is an architect with an international reputation, but the design was condemned as ugly. The Welsh National Opera, which was to have been housed in the new building, also has a considerable reputation, but opera, it was implied, is elitist. Why should millions of pounds be spent on a project that will benefit only a handful of people?

The *Mail's* campaign was so successful that not only was Zaha Hadid's design in the end turned down, the project itself was shelved. In place of the proposed opera house, Cardiff got a new rugby venue, the Millennium Stadium, where the nation's *chanteuse* Shirley Bassey, wearing a dress made out of the Welsh flag, entertained an enthusiastic crowd.

What *The Western Mail* failed to see is that a prestigious project like an opera house designed by a major architect can become a focal point for a city, repositioning it in the new Europe – as Frank Gehry's Guggenheim Museum of Modern and Contemporary Art has done for Bilbao. Moreover, opera audiences in Wales are not as uniform as the *Mail's* campaign implied. When I worked as a tutor for the Open University in Cardiff in the mid 1980s, a number of students from a variety of backgrounds, including a foreman at the Llanwern Steelworks, were keen opera-goers. Far from being elitist, opera for them was an exciting part of everyday life. Few of them I'd guess had much money, but tickets, they said, could be picked up comparatively cheaply.

Cardiff also turned down the opportunity to host the UK Year of Literature and Writing in 1995; as one city councillor is reported to have said, "There aren't any Welsh writers apart from Dylan Thomas, are there?" Instead, it was taken on by Swansea who organised a very successful year-long series of events.

Cardiff is an instructive example. It has the Millennium Centre, which is a striking new building, but for the rest the city centre is being turned into a series of massive shopping malls occupied by the same glossy chain stores that can be found in the same style of mall in every city in Britain. The architecture is undistinguished. The end result is the commodification of life that is as drab in its way as anything imposed under the old Communist regimes of Eastern Europe.

A viable culture in a complex modern society ought to be complex itself, with many variables. If it is a liberal culture one of its ideals ought to be the opening up of high culture to as many people as possible. This is what *access* to the arts used to mean, for even art that is considered difficult or by tradition the prerogative of the educated middle class can be made available to many if it is presented in the right way. When I taught poetry classes for the Workers' Educational Association in Ebbw Vale and Pontypool and for the Open University in Cardiff in the 1980s I was left with a strong impression of the keenness of the participants, of their pleasure in a wide range of poets and poems, and of the diversity of their backgrounds, from steelworkers and ex-miners to secretaries, farmers, and professional musicians. The WEA, the Open University, and extra-mural departments (as they used to be known) in universities, were all founded with this ideal of spreading the achievements of the humanities and the arts as widely as possible.

That ideal has been lost sight of. Academics themselves, especially in literature departments, have retreated behind Theory and its esoteric idiom that is only accessible to the initiated. In the process, poems and novels have been reduced to "texts" that are ancillary to impenetrable, programmatic studies that no one reads outside the academy. It is an ultimate form of bad writing, eschewing clarity, and desensitised as to why poets and novelists write, and why ordinary people have been drawn to read them. Students are encouraged to write about literature in the same way because that is how to get a good degree. Anyone with a love of literature should avoid English departments, study something else and read in their spare time.

Under conditions in which language is eroded into unintelligibility by academics, and into doublespeak by politicians and administrators, it is unsurprising that the concept of access to the arts has come to mean the opposite of opening up the achievements of high culture to as many people as possible. Instead it means the promotion of what might be called participatory arts where as many people as possible are encouraged to join in and where it is frequently difficult to tell who are the artists and who is the audience.

There has always been, and is now, room for the amateur artist and participation in the arts at an amateur level; but in an age when arts funding is overwhelmingly in the hands of the government and disbursed through its agencies, the arts councils; when governments subscribe to the Thatcherite sleight of hand that they are divesting themselves of centralised control and delivering choice to the people; when the arts and the humanities can be dismissed by government ministers for not being utilitarian enough – or in a twist on this, when they are measured by how much they contribute to the national economy; in such an age, the arts can be manipulated by the giving and withholding of government money, and high art forms that are also expensive, like opera and ballet, can be brought under suspicion, if not disrepute, on the grounds that their "products" are elitist.

There has of course been resistance to this trend, in Wales as in England, and in Wales we have been lucky in that, under the umbrella of the Welsh Books Council, literature at least has managed to stay clear of its worst effects for the time being. Financial pressure is a constant consideration, however. Since

Thatcher came to power, successive governments have shown their indifference to, if not contempt for, the arts by squeezing them of funds, so that more and more difficult choices have had to be made by arts councils and other funding agencies. To gain breathing space it is tempting for funding bodies to show their credentials by financing participatory art, people's art, at the expense of high art which under present conditions can never escape from the damning charge of elitism.

According to an article in *The Western Mail* (29 March 2008) by Peter Finch, Director of Academi, there has been pressure from some quarters to remodel the Wales Book of the Year award, worth £10,000 each for the best book in Welsh and English, which is chosen annually by a panel of three judges. Why, the argument goes, should the prize be chosen by experts? Moreover, "Who picked the judges? And why? Shouldn't best be the most popular, the best selling, the one that gets into most homes? Why are we hung up here with literary quality?" In the article, Peter Finch remains agnostic on the issue. The situation may easily change, however, if the Assembly Government seizes on the prize as an easy means of responding to the *vox populi*.

Junk culture is roomy, forever expanding its realm, and it does not care whether, as a consequence, "Universal Darkness buries All".

THE MONSTER IN THE ROOM

I heard Sorley Maclean read once in a seminar room at Copenhagen University. At the time I knew nothing of his poetry; nor did most of the other ten or so people who turned up. He introduced each poem in English before reading it in Gaelic, followed by his own translation. The translation was almost super-fluous. Sorley Maclean read in a high style with a keening delivery that emphasised the mellifluousness of the Scots Gaelic language. When he read a poem like "Dol an Iar" (Going Westwards), about his experience of the desert campaign in North Africa during the Second World War, the Gaelic had a physical effect on me – a shivery prickling of the skin. I knew from the introduction that the poem was a lament for the futility of war that traced a path from the Western Isles through Belsen and Dachau to the dead Nazi soldiers he encountered in the desert. With this knowledge, Sorley Maclean's reading of the Gaelic was enough. The poem commu-nicated itself beyond the surface meaning of the words, and the translation that followed was a winding down from the intensity of the original.

R.S. Thomas, too, had what might be called an archaic deliv-ery. Like Sorley Maclean, he belonged to a generation of poets who still believed that the difference between poetry and prose should be articulated in the reading of it. Sorley Maclean had a warmer personality than R.S. Thomas, or so it seemed to me, yet when they stood up to read, they shared a remoteness from their audience, wrapped up in the poetry for which they were merely the vehicle. What mattered was the poem, not the personality. Sorley Maclean's introductions gave essential information, at times in an impassioned way, about the experience that informed his poems, but it was as if he were talking into the distance. R.S. Thomas rarely gave any introductions at all.

This is very different from most poets today. In contemporary society, "personality" and "personal experience" are everything, and poets tend to adapt their readings accordingly. It is common for a poet to invest as much in the introduction to a poem, for example, as in the poem itself, building the reading into a minor autobiography, accentuating the experience behind the poem in order to gain rapport with the audience, to suggest the poet's essential ordinariness. And audiences like this. Many members of an audience are would-be poets themselves and this rubbing out of the distinction between poet and audience, the delivery of the poem as if it were hardly more than an extension of the introduction, creates an atmosphere of fellow-feeling; the poet is just "one of us" who happens to have stepped up to the microphone. Poetry is homely, demotic, and anyone can do it if they really try.

The relationship of the poet to the poem is not straightforward, however. A poem is "by" Sorley Maclean or "by" R.S. Thomas in the sense that it emerged from the poet's mind and his hand wrote it. This is acknowledged on title pages and in the laws governing copyright. In a deeper sense, however, the poem does not belong to the poet. It is true that the poem has a particular locus in the complex experience of one individual and that the work of every great poet has a unique stamp to it. It is also true that there is a strong craft element in poetry, and that the poet is a handyman who gets up his characteristic style through years of experiment and discarded try-outs. At the deepest level, though, the poet does not control his material. Most often, when he sits down with a blank sheet of paper and a pencil, or the blank page of a computer screen, he will not know what he is going to write. He may have a verse form in mind, because stumbling on a new form is often the start of a creative run which ends only when the form has become exhausted. Then the poet finds himself writing "Parnassian" verse, composed in his style but lacking organic integrity. When a poet is writing at full stretch, however, he is not writing the poem, the poem is being written through him – the poet is the vehicle for the poem rather than its author. The poem, it is true, draws on the poet's experience for subject matter and imagery, but these will be taken from quite disparate elements in the poet's life and often from aspects of it that he did not think important, that he caught, as it were, out of the corner of his eye.

This is what makes life exciting for the poet. Each sitting down at the desk is a fishing excursion, with the mind a lake of unknown depth. Often nothing is caught and the poet gets up empty handed to get through the day as best he can. Then, next day, there is the same intent listening and, if he is lucky, a phrase, an image emerges out of the lake which, as soon as it is written down, takes on a life of its own. Composition after that is often rapid. It is not automatic writing exactly, but it is a kind of dictation from deep within the poet over which he has minimal control. In fact, a promising start can be ruined by the poet attempting to take over, second guessing what is to come and ending with the desiccated husk of Parnassian verse. There may be revision afterwards, but when a poem emerges it is a surprise to the poet, often on a theme he would not have contemplated, and with imagery of a kind he could not have "thought up". The conscious mind produces the calculated tropes of rhetoric; the deeper, richer seams of metaphor, simile and symbol in poetry emerge from somewhere beyond consciousness.

A poem is therefore a form of exploration as much for the poet as for the reader. The poet *is* indeed a reader of his own work once it is on the page and in one important sense it is as if it has been written by someone else. If a finished poem does not have this sense of discovery for the poet, then it is probably not a good poem.

This is where the poet as monster comes in. The moments of creation are far between; weeks and months can go by as he sits each morning at the desk, and nothing comes. Eventually the poet says to himself that he will take a break, and for weeks he does other things. But no matter how enjoyable or necessary, almost everything else he does is diversionary from the main task which is to write; for it is the next poem which haunts him, which is there in the depths of the mind, and which he must move towards stealthily.

If left to himself the poet can live, submerged as it were, with his secret. But in the modern world we cannot leave him alone. We too are on a fishing expedition to haul in this beast and make him perform before us. So the most successful authors do the rounds of the big literature festivals each summer, sometimes reading from their work, but more often "in conversation with", when they are expected to rehearse their lives, the genesis of their books, their ideas on literature and politics.

It can be argued that no writer has to perform in this way. Under present conditions, however, there is great pressure on him to do so from publishers and the reading public. Being a presence at literary events, being profiled in the Saturday and Sunday supplements, sells more books than serious reviews. Moreover, all this extra-literary activity, including for some a tenured post in a prestigious Department of Creative Writing, brings in more money than royalties could ever do.

There is also vanity. The process of writing and publishing is, by its nature, an isolating one. The book is published, is on the shelves for a few months, is reviewed; yet it is as if nothing has happened. Appearing on stage before a sea of faces ready to applaud, eager to have books signed, is a physical validation of what the writer has done; the applause at the end of his perform-ance is the music of success. It is also a drug that draws him on and on until the writer becomes a parody of himself; an actor pretending to be a writer.

Robinson Jeffers understood this well. "If God has been good enough to give you a poet", he wrote in "Let Them Alone",

> Then listen to him. But for God's sake let him alone until
>   he is dead; no prizes, no ceremony,
> They kill the man. A poet is one who listens
> To nature and his own heart; and if the noise of the world
>   grows up around him, and if he is tough enough,
> He can shake off his enemies but not his friends.
> That is what withered Wordsworth and muffled Tennyson,
>   and would have killed Keats; that is what makes
> Hemingway play the fool and Faulkner forget his art.

Jeffers had a permanent sign outside Tor House, his home in

California, that read *Not at Home*.

Jeffers' warning has not been listened to, of course – a fact that would not have surprised him. Far from leaving the poet alone, we have invited him to become a dancing bear. "Do it again!" an audience cries, and the bear obliges. On occasion, though, he balks. At a reading in Lampeter, a member of the audience asked R.S. Thomas to read "A Peasant". His answer was a brusque "No". It seemed rude at the time, and R.S. Thomas could appear rude; yet in retrospect I think it was a defence mechanism. The bear was rebelling, pulling against the chain and refusing to dance.

Left to themselves, poets can merge with the crowd. I once drove past R.S. Thomas standing on a street corner in Pwllheli, supermarket plastic bag in hand. Like Robinson Jeffers, his features were distinctive; yet to passers-by he was just a gaunt old man. Poets need that ordinariness to shield their secret, the monstrous compunction that makes them fish again and again in the mind's shadowy lake. By making them perform in public, by making them explain themselves, we force them out of that cover. But the applause we give represents a failure to understand that it is the poem that counts, not the poet; that once the poem has been written and published it has, in the truest sense, nothing more to do with its author; and that the self-consciousness we foist upon him is the surest way to destroy the poet's art, leaving him maimed.

SURVEILLANCE

When I read George Orwell's *Nineteen Eighty-Four* as a teenager, I thought the idea of a screen that monitored every individual in the privacy of his or her home was part of a fantasy future that could never happen. Half a century on, I am not so sure. Recently, as my train pulled into Birmingham New Street at the end of its journey from London, I stood in the corridor near an exit door. Idly looking around as the train slowed, I noticed a sign informing passengers that we were under CCTV surveillance for our own "safety and security". I couldn't see anything that looked like a camera, however, and a fellow passenger, a Londoner, who read the notice at the same time was equally puzzled. We pooled our resources and came to the conclusion that the camera must have been inside a small black half-sphere above our heads. The Londoner speculated that from the time he walked out of his house until he entered the building where his meeting was to be in Birmingham (and probably within the building itself, since it was a business meeting) he would have been monitored by CCTV. The police or the security services, if they wished, could have followed his movements throughout the journey.

It is hard to comprehend the scale of surveillance in contemporary Britain. Even in a small town like Aberystwyth, CCTV cameras that you hardly notice follow you on the main streets. You cannot enter a supermarket or a large pub or a public building, or wait for a train, without being filmed.

In 1958 it seemed far-fetched that Winston Smith, the protagonist of *Nineteen Eighty-Four*, had to take a trip into the countryside to be sure that he was unobserved by the State. In

2010 it seems less so. But then Winston was a rebel against the State; he had something to hide. Merely by seeking to evade surveillance he was guilty of a crime – if, that is, you accept the rationale of the system.

And it is such a rationale that we are being urged to accept now. Surveillance is for our own good, as public notices routinely inform us – with the unwritten corollary that only the guilty could object to being caught on film. For the State is benevolent. In establishing and maintaining such an expensive surveillance system it is thinking only of us, the ordinary citizens who have nothing to hide and therefore nothing to fear. The system is searching for bad apples and when these are identified by security guards or the police, they are plucked from the endless stream of the masses whose grey ordinariness is on display day and night on countless arrays of monitors.

At the moment CCTV only records images, but it may not be long before it also records sound so that those who are watching will also be able to listen in to our conversations. Again we will be assured that the State is only interested in identifying wrong-doers, or those acting suspiciously, or suspects whom the police or the intelligence services need to keep under surveillance.

It was the same with the now abandoned Identity Card. Far from being a diminution of the individual's freedom, we were told, it would be an advantage because it would make it easier to identify ourselves on the occasions when this was necessary. So too with iris recognition, fingerprinting, DNA banks – all these means of compiling information about the individual that are with us or on the horizon; their only purpose is to make our world safer. This is still some way from surveillance in the home, though inroads have been made here, too, with the introduction of electronic tagging for petty criminals and suspects, whose every move can be monitored from the local police station. Some form of tagging for the nation by means of a microchip implant may be only a few decades away.

Many accept surveillance in public places on the basis of the argument that CCTV helps to reduce crime, or, if it doesn't exactly do that, helps the police to solve crime after the event. There is a problem with surveillance, however, which the State is not so interested in discussing, and that is the way in which extensive monitoring changes the balance between the individual and the State. This is always under negotiation. The State in a complex modern society is by nature centralist; it not only accrues power to itself where it can, it also seeks to place limits on the freedom of the individual by channelling the activities of citizens toward State-approved ends.

When, therefore, a government declares that its policy is to devolve power to the individual by providing greater freedom of choice in areas such as health and education, we should be on our guard. The State only talks up freedom and choice when it wishes to introduce policies that diminish them. By the same token, when it emphasises the advantages to the citizen of surveillance, we should consider the disadvantages.

It is easy enough to foresee a situation in which, for example, a political party with a racist agenda gains power through democratic election. For such a party, a nation-wide surveillance system, combined with a database of all citizens and compulsory ID cards, would be invaluable for any pogroms it chose to initiate.

More important for now, however, is the way in which mass surveillance subtly undermines our status as individuals even though we may hardly be aware of it. Catch a glimpse of yourself on the overhead screen as you enter a supermarket, or as you stand in line at a bank or building society, and you become objectified. The camera forces you to see yourself from the outside, one of thousands – in a big city one of millions – reduced to a matter of record, a matter of externals. You contemplate yourself as a stranger – just as the anonymous watcher at the array of screens sees you. You may argue that this does not matter, that you know who you are, on the inside. Yet it may be that those tribespeople had a point who believed that taking their photographs stole something of their spirit.

Our kind of society dislikes individuality and independent thought. In its place it has substituted personality as that is understood by the tabloids, by magazines like *Hello!* and *OK!*, and increasingly by what used to be the broadsheets. Personality in this sense is a world of photographic surfaces. What you see is what you get, and what you get is very little.

Surveillance feeds off this world in interesting ways. The omnipresence of digital cameras, mobile phones that record images, and camcorders, means that we are constantly photographing ourselves as well as one another; constantly seeing ourselves as photographic objects. The habit is so extensive that for many, a photographic record of an event is more real than the event itself. Photography validates us. Yet it only validates surfaces, reducing us to two-dimensional images, or two-dimensional images in a fourth-dimensional time-loop if it is film. The ubiquity of such self-documentation is a kind of voluntary surveillance, in which the inner life is less important than the objectified externals.

Andy Warhol famously said that in contemporary society everyone gets his or her fifteen minutes of fame. The multiplication of digital television channels and with them of viewer-participation programmes, and programmes like *Big Brother*, *The Weakest Link* and *The Apprentice*, as well as countless "fly on the wall" documentaries, have given his words greater resonance than he could have imagined. And if you are so unlucky as not to have appeared on television, you can create your own "programme" on the internet through a personal website, or a blog, or by logging on to Facebook or MySpace.

In such a culture, even appearing on CCTV can give a *frisson*, so it is no surprise to learn from a recent report that far from discouraging violent street crime, CCTV cameras may actually encourage it among teenagers, as if the presence of the cameras validates the deed, even though the only time they are likely to see the recorded film is in a court of law.

This urge to objectify the self through the image explains, at least in part, why there has been no significant opposition to the proliferation of surveillance in public places. It is seen merely as an extension of what people do among themselves on a day-to-day basis. Looking up to watch yourself on-screen as you walk into a supermarket seems natural – this is me, walking into the supermarket – even though the purpose of the prominently placed monitor is to remind you that inside the store there will be other cameras that you do not see and other monitors following your every move as you weigh-up the vegetables or lift out a plastic tray of meat.

For the same reason, the proposed Identity Card failed to engender widespread opposition. There was an organisation, No2ID, whose members pledged to go to prison rather than comply, but there was unlikely to have been protest on the scale of the anti-Poll Tax movement of the 1980s which forced Margaret Thatcher to back down and withdraw the tax.

This is not merely because people are more concerned about government measures that affect their income. It is because modern surveillance by the State has developed from the same technology which, in the mass market, encourages voluntary objectification by the individual. The purposes are different but the digitised outcome can seem the same, or at least so similar that the trivial nature of the one obscures the seriousness of the other.

Where do we go from here? The new technology is helping to prize free the mortar of shared interests that are the basis for a democratic society, replacing it with a loose agglomeration of individuals. Used to seeing ourselves in objectified terms, we are the more easily manipulated by the State and by market consumerism which is so integral to it that we ought to think in terms of the Business State. Under these conditions, political engagement is in danger of atrophying, which in turn encourages the extension of State control over our lives. But the latent anomie of contemporary society is also fertile ground for the demagogue, the "man of vision", who settles on a single grievance – it might be immigration – and whips this into a powerful political force, for which neither the State in its present form, nor the democratic structures which it is busily undermining, are prepared.

DEEP DOWN IN THE JUNGLE

As we destroy the last of the Earth's rain forests we are busy creating a virtual one, the World Wide Web. There explorers can hack trails deeper and deeper into its mass. Type in "the poetry of R.S. Thomas", for example, or "plate tectonics", and you can spend weeks or months following trails that branch and branch, then branch again, sometimes in what appears to be an endless profusion – except that you can only glimpse a few of these trails at a time; the electronic foliage, as it were, closes silently behind you, as you travel on. It is true that you can turn back to traverse previously explored ground, but not always, for sometimes a site that looked like a sturdy tree has crashed into electronic oblivion.

Deep in the jungle, too, are shanty towns and even extensive cities where millions of individuals peer out of personal websites, and bloggers jostle for attention like carpet sellers in bazaars, each with his or her little booth, peddling trivia or ignorance, opinion or analysis.

There is one area where very few people go. It is the Dismal Swamp, and nobody knows its extent. There, if you dared, you would find terrorists, paedophiles, purveyors of violence and horror, snuff movies even. The police and the secret services patrol there, watching and listening. If you were to enter, you might wake up to the crash of your front door as it is battered down and armed men run up the stairs.

Compasses are of little use in the forest. An intellectual compass with T for Truth spins violently as you advance. Almost everything appears to be true or claims to be; but how is it possible you know? Wikipedia is said to be the encyclopaedia of encyclopaedias. Anyone can make an entry on any subject and the entry is then updated and purged of error by other users. The result is the best up-to-date information on almost any topic you can think of. If a malicious user inserts false information, it will be spotted by others and corrected. But when you click on an entry, how do you know what its status is at that moment? The malicious contributor may just have inserted his misinformation and there may not have been time for another user to correct it. Wikipedia has even had to close entries temporarily because they had become so corrupted. Other sites claiming to purvey factual information are equally open to suspicion. A friend forwarded to me a site entry which listed the books I have published. Half the books were said to have appeared in two editions, yet none of my books has been reprinted let alone gone into a second edition. The site was a factual one, yet significant facts were wrong.

Print has its own problems and limitations, of course. Information in a print encyclopaedia can become dated very quickly and it might be many years before a revised, updated edition is published. Errors can also creep into print editions. But a team of experienced editors, contributions from acknowledged experts, and publication by a major publishing house are a better guarantee of accuracy than anonymous entries on the Net that may be altered and honed by many hands, any one of whom may be a trickster.

There are futuristic techno-dreamers who claim that the age of the book is dead or at least dying; that the future for literature, for literary journals, for print culture in general, is electronic. It is not only computer engineers and programmers who think like this; there are writers who, believing they have signed up to the future, belittle the culture of print. When you hear them talk or read their columns on the subject you can sense the thrill this gives them. The last generation of book readers will soon be dead, they say, and then the world of electronic culture will come into its own.

In *Star Trek: The Next Generation*, Jean-Luc Picard, Captain of *The Enterprise*, is presented as a man of culture. He has a strong interest in inter-planetary archaeology and a small but well-chosen collection of artefacts from ancient sites across the galaxy. He is also a reader with a penchant for literature and history, and often appears off duty in his quarters reading from a hand-held computer "book". Usually, it is clear from the context, this is something factual – a report from Star Fleet Headquarters, perhaps.

But Captain Picard also has a collection of real books, hardbacked, sometimes with leather spines, that look as if they were published in the nineteenth century and so would be considered antiquarian, seen from our time or his. These are what he reads for pleasure. In this he is unusual. The rest of his officers are not readers. Some of them take part in, or attend, a classical concert now and then, but mostly they prefer to relax on the holodeck, or in the dimly lit lounge bar where they sip brightly coloured drinks, to remind us that this is the future and they are far from home.

In one episode, Picard is travelling by shuttle to a base where he is to undergo heart surgery. The journey is slow and to pass the time he reads a large-format book while the shuttle is piloted by his young protégé, Ensign Wesley Crusher. A light and easily held computer-book would have been far more convenient, but out there in the immensity of deep space, Picard reads a print book from a time long ago.

It would be easy to dismiss him as an antiquarian with a harmless but irrelevant interest in the past and its outdated print technology. Picard might even seem pretentious, holding out for old-fashioned ways when everyone knows that the electrobook is the reality. But that is not how he is presented in the series, for he is the captain of Star Fleet's flagship, *au fait* with the latest technologies, and he is not pretentious but modest and thoughtful.

The book in Picard's hands represents something which the makers of *Star Trek* understand but which the literary techno-prophets of our time seek to deny: that a book is more than the words on the page. In book form, a novel or a collection of poems has a physicality which is deeply appealing to humans because we are sensuous beings. The feel of a page, the design of a dust wrapper, the smell even of a new book, its weight in the hand, the act of turning a page as you read, are all part of the literary experience which is three-dimensional and tactile as well as intellectual and emotional. Reading a book on-screen, or calling it up on a miniaturised, hand-held computer, negates these non-literary but essentially human aspects of the reading process. The literary technos don't care about this, however, as they stare into the future and predict the downfall of the book in excited tones.

And it may be that they will have their way. Librarians are notoriously busy off-loading books and installing computers in their place, for it is the future we must hurry into, whereas libraries in their traditional form are archives of the past. I was at a meeting in the English Department at Swansea University not long ago. It took place in a small but very well selected Department library. I commented on this and was told by a member of staff that, yes, it was a good library, largely due to the bequest of a former professor, but that unfortunately it had to go because the university administration had decreed that the room was needed for... administration.

Meanwhile, back in the jungle, the explorer is constantly under attack from spam, the insect life of the electroforest teaming in its millions and catering to every form of desire from penis enlargement to designer watches. And then there are the viruses whose malicious purpose is to damage or destroy what you have carefully stored, merely for the pleasure of it, without having met you or even knowing who you are.

Everything appears to be on the Net, and if you could survey it in some all-encompassing way, it might be possible to draw significant conclusions about what humanity is. But that is impossible. The Net grows exponentially – or at least that is a reasonable assumption; great trees of knowledge and evil arise from an undergrowth of trivia and egotism in this pixilated forest and when they fall, new growth scrambles onto the screen to take their place. It is chaotic and provisional, and comprehensible only in fragments. The great age of geographical exploration in the real world has been over for some time. In that sense the Earth has shrunk and we have lost forever the thrill of the unknown that used to be out there behind the forest wall, beyond the deep blue mountains. The need to explore is a driving force in humans, however, and we seem to have diverted it very successfully into the Net. For the electroforest is without limit; we can wander through it night and day, losing ourselves for hours in the twists and turns of its paths, before heading back, powering down, to emerge once more into the light of four-dimensional reality, the coffee cup at our hand, a wind gusting in the bushes outside the window.

WE'RE ALL VOYEURS NOW

Originally, the term *voyeur* had a limited sexual connotation; a voyeur was someone who became aroused while watching clandestinely as other people had sex. In recent usage, though, it has enlarged its meaning to include any situation in which an individual gains satisfaction, sexual or otherwise, from looking on as others expose themselves physically or psychologically. This has always been a facet of the tabloid press, but it has come into its own in the past decade with the invention and proliferation of "reality" TV and the ubiquity of mobile phones that can record moving images. There is an added twist to contemporary voyeurism. In its earlier, more limited usage, the term implied that those being watched were unaware of the fact; this was part of the excitement for the voyeur. Today, more often than not, there is a knowing collusion between the voyeur and those being viewed; the latter actively seeking exposure, from which they themselves gain an exhibitionist thrill.

Voyeurism and exhibitionism have been brought together in a compulsive way in popular television, so that thousands apply to take part in programmes like *Big Brother* and *The Apprentice*, and millions watch them. (It might be argued that the lure of *The Apprentice* is the prospect of a £100,000 post in Alan Sugar's corporation. While this is true, an equally significant factor is likely to be the opportunity to expose yourself on television in the rows and confrontations, the backbiting and bullying, that are part of the programme's dynamics.)

Such programmes reflect social trends and preoccupations, but they also act as positive feedback loops that exaggerate and perpetuate them. And what they perpetuate is a low, if not the lowest, common denominator. In this they are abetted by the tabloids who report and comment on the programmes as they unfold, picking up on viewers' reactions to individual contestants, especially the unpopular ones who they turn into hate figures. In this way, a complete unknown like Jade Goody can become a household name overnight, her photograph in all the papers, her appearance and behaviour picked over for praise or preferably vilification. For what reality TV is predicated on is conflict and humiliation, and this is what the tabloids also do best. Jade Goody became an unlikely TV and tabloid star for a while, groomed and promoted, even launching her own perfume. But when she got in a spat with an Indian starlet on *Big Brother* and in a fit of temper abused her racially, Goody was pilloried and brought tumbling down. The voyeuristic element in all this was the evident delight with which the media destroyed her while cynically pretending to righteous indignation. Jade Goody became a national figure of hate, even though in most respects she was no better or worse than the viewers of *Big Brother*. She was ordinary and working class, propelled into a situation in which she was out of her depth, in which her normal behaviour became exaggeratedly grotesque because of its context. Her ordinariness was part of the fascination; any one could have taken her place but she had been chosen. Envy in millions of living rooms as much as anything else contributed to her fall.

Jade Goody, however, had one last card up her sleeve. In 2009, she let it be known that she had terminal cancer, and in what was an unusual *volte-face* for the tabloids, she was re-admitted to tabloid heaven. Portraits of her, head bald from chemotherapy, filled the front pages, and when she announced that she was marrying her boyfriend before she died, the tabloids were in ecstasy. "What Brave Star Told Her Little Boy", was the front page subheading in *The News of the World* on the eve of the wedding. And indeed Jade Goody *was* a star again, in junk culture terms, whose predicament could be exploited on all sides. Max Clifford, her publicist, negotiated a £1 million wedding photo exclusive with a television channel and a magazine. Everyone else, including the BBC and what used to be the broadsheets, felt impelled to report on this media-created event as best they could. As I have suggested, gross sentimentality and hatred are the Janus face of the tabloids. Jade Goody ran the gamut from one to the other and, amazingly, back again, but the asking price was her death.

Moral judgements hover over reality TV, but they are rarely brought into play. *The Apprentice* is predicated on the assumption that big business is a good thing and that we are all aspiring entrepreneurs. Week by week over the three-month run of the programme, we watch as contestants are whittled down, "fired" for their inadequacies in the final humiliating scene in Sugar's garish boardroom with its underlit glass table. The ultimate winner is only partly the one who shows the most entrepreneurial flair in the various tasks. He or she is also the one who is most successful in plotting against rivals; who can best demonstrate ruthlessness in the pursuit of business success – like the contestant who, in the gruelling interviews toward the end of each series, boasted that he had no qualms about making a forty-year-old father of two small children redundant at his previous company. It had been necessary for the good of the corporation which he put before all other considerations. Gray's tyrant who "shut the gates of mercy on mankind" comes to mind, but the man's cold-heartedness was not commented on in any of the newspaper reports that I read.

Reality TV is relentless in its pursuit of situations in which individuals expose their worst sides, playing the exhibitionist on flat screens in millions of homes. There is nothing "real" about it, since contestants in programmes like *Big Brother* are chosen with the aim of creating an explosive mix. Where would the fun be if everyone was amicable? Reality TV pushes continuously at the boundaries of the acceptable, because we, the audience, are insatiable for more. What will Jade Goody do next? How outrageous will she be? Fascination, adoration and hate are mixed into the brew. It is a question as to where the final boundaries are. A sudden and savage fight between two aggressive males? A murder? Sex in "the house" is already passé.

The voyeuristic credentials of reality TV have spread beyond the boundaries of the genre in recent years and infected news programmes. It is now common on all channels to interview the bereaved, whether it is the parents of a murdered teenager or the family of a soldier killed in Iraq or Afghanistan. "She was such a lovely girl," a father says through his tears about his soldier-daughter; "her smile conquered everyone." With the exception, an objective viewer might think, of the Taliban who killed her. But we are not encouraged to think like that; we are meant to sit back with a vague sympathetic thrill – "How awful!"

There is certainly reality here – the grieving with their tear-stained, hopeless faces. Yet what purpose does such an interview serve as an item of news? Some parents of dead soldiers refuse the bait of a television appearance where they are expected to parade their grief for the benefit of viewers. Yet many agree. It is an ultimate form of exhibitionism and an ultimate form of voyeurism, though the relatives can perhaps be excused in that, in the confusion of their grieving, there was little time to reflect on what they were being asked to do.

But the producers and directors do know what they are asking, as does the cameraman as he peers into the lens, slowly panning closer to the crying face. This is *real* suffering, not the pretence of television drama where no matter how much we are caught up in the action we know it is only actors acting. This is as close as it is possible to get to one of the extremes of life without suffering ourselves. Few who create news items of this sort, or who watch them, are likely to reflect that such scenes are on a sliding scale leading at the other end to the barbaric world of snuff movies.

(If you think that last point is an exaggeration, remember the mobile phone footage of Saddam Hussein's execution as, in the last seconds of his life and with the hangman's noose around his neck, he rebuked those who were mocking him, with a good deal more dignity than they had. That was shown on the news, and repeated several times. Not a snuff movie exactly, but very close.)

The demand we make on people that they should expose their feelings to the nation has a resemblance (in a distorting mirror) to the state trials of the Third Reich and Stalinist Russia. Reality there was brutal and cruel. Individuals were plucked out of their lives and interrogated under torture before "confessing" in court-room scenes that were sometimes filmed, after which they were despatched to concentration camps or murdered.

Such scenes were a precursor of reality TV, for at one level they were no more real than *Big Brother* in that charges against the accused were more often than not trumped up by the police and confessions extorted under duress. Trials were "real" in the same arranged way, with the verdict a foregone conclusion. For those involved (apart from the victims) there must have been a frisson of excitement in all this – the simulacrum of a real world in which the accused *might* have been a dangerous enemy of the state; a game in which you play interrogator, prosecutor, judge or executioner; a world where reality flickers uncertainly, and truth dies out. They were not known as show trials for nothing.

That was a deadly game with reality, of course, a long way from the ugly bickering of the participants on *Big Brother*, the petty ruthlessness of the would-be apprentices, or the televised misery of the bereaved on the national news. But there lurks behind our play with reality a confusion of moral values, and too often a willingness to set them aside. What kind of a world is it where a young man presents as a qualification for a post in management the fact that he has no problem sacking an older, more vulnerable colleague? A world where you can sit back in an easy chair and watch the bereaved as they confess through tears their loss and their grief?

Even if you do not watch reality TV, its amoral, voyeuristic mix cannot be avoided entirely. It jumps out at you in news bulletins; it permeates once serious newspapers like *The Independent*. One day, there may be a knock on your door, and you will open it to the cameraman in his anorak, and the interviewer in his suit, a hand reaching out toward you, not in sympathy, but with a microphone.

PANIC ATTACK

In the 1970s I was a fan of disaster movies like *The Towering Inferno* and *The Poseidon Adventure*. I watched them uncritically, and no doubt like everyone else in the cinema, felt a certain *schadenfreude* at the destruction of the massive skyscraper through human folly and greed, or the sight of *S.S. Poseidon*, the luxury cruise liner, as it was rolled over by a tsunami, like a child's toy. Yet although they involved much destruction and loss of life, they were in the end optimistic films, as Hollywood films usually are, about the triumph of humanity. They were at once warnings against hubris, cautionary tales about the limits of technology, and stories of individual heroism and survival as the world caves in around you.

In all this they were dry runs for the destruction of the World Trade Center in 2001. Watching the planes crash into the towers, watching the towers blaze and collapse; people running and screaming in the streets; the terrible smack of bodies hitting the pavement as men and women flung themselves in desperation from the towers' windows; then learning later of the bravery and self-sacrifice of the firefighters; the stupidity of some executives who ordered staff to remain at their desks – it was impossible not to think "*Towering Inferno*".

But the destruction of the Twin Towers took place in the real world; a world, moreover, that was significantly different from the 1970s when the disaster films were made. For during the 1990s and the first decade of the present century, optimism of the will, which was central to the ethos of the disaster movies, has been replaced in Anglo-American culture by a low-level angst that finds expression in periodic bouts of mass hysteria. These are often fanned, if not actually created, by the media. But journalists are only of their times, and in reporting the kind of hypothetical scenario that triggers the panics, they are merely responding to a malaise in society that is already there.

The strain of bird flu known as H5N1 is a good example. Avian flu is a virulent disease endemic in wild bird populations, especially in South-East Asia, and millions of birds die from it each year. It spreads easily to poultry, and to date some 200 million farm birds have been slaughtered in efforts to contain it, at an estimated loss of $10 billion. In 2005 an outbreak of H5N1 spread rapidly from South-East Asia to China, through Pakistan and Turkey, and into Europe. Bird flu has been known to jump the species barrier and infect and kill other species of animal, and when poultry workers in Asia became infected and some of them died, there was a real fear of a pandemic among humans that nobody was prepared for. David Nabarro, the United Nations Chief Asian Flu Co-ordinator, warned that up to 150 million people could die worldwide. The nearest thing to a vaccine, marketed under the brand name Tamiflu, inhibits the spread of the disease in the human body, but stocks were nowhere near sufficient if a pandemic was about to take place.

The spread of the virus was front-page news; maps with threatening arrows showed the migration paths of wild birds from Asia to Europe; the slaughter of poultry was plotted country by country as the flu spread; human deaths among poultry workers in Asia were highlighted; people stopped eating chicken for fear of catching H5N1 from birds that couldn't possibly have been infected. The stories continued on the inside pages for several weeks.

And then they faded away, because as far as a pandemic among humans was concerned, nothing happened. In fact, between 2003 and 2008 only 385 people have been known to contract bird flu worldwide, out of whom 243 have died. That is a high percentage, and suggests that if a strain of bird flu were to evolve which was highly contagious in our own species, then the death toll might be proportionally high. It appears, however, that H5N1 was not that strain, and David Nabarro has been accused of alarmism for pulling the figure of 150 million deaths out of a hat. To date, no one has died from the disease in Europe.

Bird flu is clearly a potential threat to humans, and governments and the UN were right to take precautions and to warn of the consequences if an outbreak occurred that spread rapidly through the human population. What is relevant here is the way in which the media developed the story. It could have been reported seriously but in a restrained way. Instead hypothetical scenarios were ratcheted up so that what was possible became probable, until in the eyes of many, the pandemic was poised at the borders of Europe, and every dead swan, every farm bird that had to be slaughtered, heralded the worst.

The media were responding to the need we currently have in the West for apocalyptic visions of death and destruction in which there is no get-out for the virtuous, because in a secular, materialist world, devastation, when it comes, will sweep us all away, the good, the bad, and the ordinary.

Disasters like the tsunami that devastated Aceh in Sumatra or the destruction of New Orleans by Hurricane Katrina might seem to satisfy this need. Certainly the media dwelt on them for a long time and in great detail. But no matter how destructive they were, these were local affairs, and do not fit the requirement for what might be called the panic-visions of the West. For what is desired is fear of the truly catastrophic in which civilisation itself is in the balance.

The best example of this is the scare story about near-Earth asteroids that was reported widely in the media a few years ago. Near-Earth asteroids have orbits that bring them close to the Earth and astronomers have been compiling a catalogue of them and monitoring their trajectories for some time. To date over 5000 have been identified.

The Earth is under constant bombardment from asteroids. Asteroids with a diameter of 5 to 10 metres crash into the atmosphere about once a year; larger asteroids with a diameter of 50 metres do so about every 1000 years. Those with a diameter of 1 kilometre or more – the serious ones – hit the Earth approximately once every 10 million years. Between 500 and 1000 of these large asteroids have been catalogued, including one known as 1950 DA which, in 2001, came within 7 to 8 million miles of the Earth. In astronomical terms, that is very close.

The asteroid that crashed into what is now the Yucatán Peninsula 65 million years ago was much bigger – perhaps 10 kilometres in diameter. Its effects were so damaging to the biosphere that an estimated 64 per cent of all species became extinct, including of course the dinosaurs. With a diameter of 1 kilometre, 1950 DA would not be so devastating, but it would be devastating enough to disrupt life on Earth severely, with disastrous consequences for humanity.

The near miss was taken up by the media and made into a scare story. There were reports of American plans to deploy rockets armed with nuclear warheads to disperse asteroids on a collision course with Earth; monitoring of near-Earth asteroids was to be stepped up; likely scenarios were published of what might have happened *had* 1950 DA crashed into the atmosphere.

The fact, however, is that 1950 DA is the one near-Earth asteroid of this diameter so far identified with an orbit that is likely to bring it on a collision course with the Earth at some point in time; and 1950 DA will not approach the Earth again until 2880, which in human terms is so far into the future that to worry about it as a risk is illogical.

The scenario of a massive asteroid impact fits too well, however, with our need for a kind of secular Book of Revelation in which, in some obscure way, we will be punished by plagues and destruction. Punished for what, is the question. Perhaps underlying these panic attacks is the half-conscious perception that things cannot go on as they are. That for all the propaganda of big business and its tools among the politicians, we have entered a labyrinth from which there may be no exit. Most of us do not want to admit this to ourselves openly – though every year there are signs of a deepening pessimism about capitalist democracy, which in turn fuels the panic and the apocalyptic angst. In this context, Cormac McCarthy's *The Road* is the quintessential novel of our times.

It explains too why religion has come into prominence again in the secularised West. Most of us in Wales may be uncommitted, but it is impossible not to be aware of the increasingly strident

voice of charismatic and evangelical Christians, whose fundamentalist version of the faith appeals to many because it seems to
make sense of what is happening. To them, we are living in the
Last Days and what we are experiencing is the fulfilment of John
the Divine's vision. For the faithful it will be all right, and if you
are a hardcore evangelical in the USA, you will be anticipating
"the Rapture" when you will be snatched up, à la *Star Trek*, in a
divine teleporter, to join the saints rejoicing around the throne.

As for the rest of us, we must find a way out of the maze as
best we can, employing reason and controlling the urge to lose
ourselves in panic and hysteria, because, *pace* the Christians, the
Earth is all we humans have, and will ever have.

COMPLEXITY AND PLANNING

Few would disagree that, at the end of the first decade of the twenty-first century, the Earth and its human population face an array of problems that are global in scale even though as individuals we may experience them locally, or in some instances (as yet) not at all. In no particular order, they include climate change, species extinction, pollution, shortage of fresh water, rainforest depletion, human overpopulation, pandemics like AIDS, and peak oil. The list could go on. Optimists will say that each can be overcome – a breakthrough in nuclear fusion will go a long way toward solving the energy crisis; overpopulation – so it has been argued – may even be a good thing, since the greater the population the greater the number of intelligent people there will be to help solve the world's problems.

The signs so far, however, are not promising. The leaders of the Western nations talk up solutions to climate change, for example, but do very little about it, as witness the Copenhagen Climate Conference in 2010. This is because people are increasingly concerned about the effects of global warming, but are unwilling to entertain radical changes in the West's affluent way of living, and the politicians know this. Under present conditions, implementing environmental policies of the kind that are necessary would be the shortest route to the Opposition benches.

Part of the problem is that the crises we face are interrelated so that it is very difficult to address them individually. The mass extinction of species, which is undoubtedly taking place, is bound up with habitat loss, especially in the tropical rainforests and coral reefs, which harbour by far the largest number of the Earth's species. To solve this problem, which may be one of the most serious for the long-term future of humans, we need to tackle global poverty, because the rainforests of Africa, South America and South-East Asia are being destroyed in part by the landless poor, desperate for a patch of earth to cultivate. The forests are also under attack, however, from logging companies, cattle ranchers whose vast estates eat deeper each year into virgin forest of the Amazon Basin, and mining corporations. Much of this is the work of multinationals reacting to, and stimulating, demand for tropical hardwoods, cheap beef, and an array of metals and minerals, especially in the West and among rapidly industrialising nations like China. Global capitalism and Western consumerism also need to be confronted, therefore, if there is to be any chance of saving what is left of the rainforests.

Deforestation in the tropics is in turn part of the positive feedback loop of global warming which is leading to a worldwide bleaching of coral reefs that are sensitive to fluctuations in ocean temperature. The death of the reefs has a huge negative impact on the numerous species of animals and plants that have evolved in close association with them.

How are we to deal with complexity and inter-relatedness of this kind? It is something humans have never faced before in our 200,000-year history. Optimists declare that solutions can be found despite the daunting nature of the problems, and optimism is always more congenial to the human race than pessimism. It may be, however, that a solution is beyond us because our brains have simply not evolved to think on the global scale that is necessary.

"Think globally, act locally" is one of the slogans of the Green movement. It is not a bad one – be aware of the overall picture and make small-scale changes in your own way of living. Little by little the overall picture itself can be changed. Much has been achieved in this way over the past ten or fifteen years. In many parts of Wales it is now possible to recycle glass, paper and cardboard, plastic bags and bottles, drinks cartons, and electrical appliances. Shoppers are becoming more aware of the source of what they buy. In almost every town in Wales there is a wholefood shop or greengrocer's that specialises in locally grown and organic produce – and they are bustling. On a local level, too, groups like

Friends of Cardigan Bay monitor wildlife and pollution in the Bay's waters; volunteers clear tons of trash each year from the beaches. A self-help world has grown up in response to what might be called mass-world – the dream of the global corporations – in which we are all herded as "consumers" into the supermarkets and megastores to buy the same over-packaged, mass-produced goods that are flown in from across the globe.

Mass-world is still dominant, however. For every individual who shops locally, there are thousands who would never dream of shopping anywhere except at the supermarket. For every family that has given up its car there are thousands who could not imagine life without one; and in many cases not just one but two, including a fashionable four-wheel-drive.

The forces that power consumer-capitalism are very effective because they appeal to an atavistic element in human nature – the instinct to gorge ourselves while we can. In evolutionary terms this made sense a hundred thousand years ago when the supply of food and raw materials was at best uncertain. The instinct is counter-productive, though, when there is always a glut and never a shortage, as is the case in the global capitalist market. The phenomenon of obesity in the developed nations should be seen in this light. Most of the grossly overweight are not "greedy" as such; they are acting on evolved aspects of human nature within the unnatural context of capitalist plenty.

This creates a problem for those who see that we need to change our way of living radically, and now. The case for controlling, and eventually dismantling, the capitalist system as it is constituted at present, is overwhelming; it is unsustainable and is propelling us toward some kind of global collapse, probably later this century, perhaps a little beyond that horizon. But the case depends on reason, and among humans that has always been in short supply. Far more attractive is the appeal to our deepest instincts; instincts that are finessed as rational choice by consumer-capitalism. At one level, it is "rational" to buy strawberries from California and asparagus from Thailand, out of season and at knock-down prices, or four factory-farmed chickens for the price of an organic one. But this is only so if we take the short-term view. In the longer term, each purchase becomes magnified by the millions of buys in other supermarkets across the developed world. We are not encouraged, however, to think in terms of the pollution of the atmosphere from the millions of air freight miles involved, or the mountains of throw-away packaging that our "choice" results in. For the "rational" element in global capitalism is in fact deeply irrational. We are sacrificing the long-term future, if not of our lives, then those of our children or grandchildren; something most of us would never do if we thought about it, yet which we do every day when we follow the false reasoning of the system we are locked into.

Reason dictates one thing, yet often we do another. The great fishing fleets of England and Scotland, using ever more refined techniques of locating shoals and netting them, combined with the fleets of Norway, Denmark, Iceland and Russia, have come close to fishing out the North Sea and the North Atlantic. Yet until quotas were introduced by the EU, an excessive number of trawlers put out to sea year after year, sailing back to harbour with ever diminishing catches. It was clear what was happening, yet many captains and owners continued in the old ways, some denying that fishing stocks were dangerously close to depletion. Seen from a long-term perspective this was deeply illogical, but in the short term many fishermen did not know what else to do. Desperation on their part, and greed on the part of the owners of the massive factory-freezer trawlers that were developed in the 1950s, meant that the extraordinarily rich cod stocks of the Grand Banks off Newfoundland were wiped out in forty years.

One feature global capitalism shares with its great twentieth-century rival, communism, is an obsession with planning. Governments like those of Tony Blair and Gordon Brown publish a new plan regulating some aspect of our lives on almost a weekly basis. But the more complex the circumstances that bear upon the plan, the more likely it is to be thwarted by the law of unintended consequences.

The attempt to control agricultural pests by introducing predators from foreign ecosystems is littered with examples. The best known is the cane toad. In the Caribbean and Hawaii this had proved effective in controlling the cane beetle. The toad is extremely poisonous, however, at all stages in its life-cycle. Let loose in the cane fields of Queensland in the 1930s it soon had a disastrous impact on all kinds of native fauna that came into contact with it. Moreover, the cane toad is a prolific breeder and has no natural predators in Australia. Within a short period of time it had spread beyond Queensland and is on a seemingly unstoppable course down the eastern seaboard.

More recently, biofuels have been promoted as a source of alternative energy and embraced by governments desperate to find solutions to the energy crisis. Farmers in the United States and elsewhere have been quick to take land out of agricultural production in response to the demand. What no one appears to have foreseen is how much land would get taken out, resulting in serious food shortages in 2008.

Under capitalism, plans involving large-scale factors, such as the need to balance food and biofuel production, appear to be difficult to execute, partly because the processes are inherently unstable. Energy production will need to be maintained at current levels, for example, if Britain's material prosperity is to continue unabated. Yet every option is loaded with difficulty. Reliance on Russia as a supplier of gas from its vast supplies leaves Britain open to political and economic pressure. Exploitation of the large reserves of coal that still exist would diminish that risk, but an increase in the number of coal-fired power stations would increase the amount of carbon we release into the atmosphere. Nuclear power – which the government is considering and which has been endorsed as a measure of desperation by Gaia-hypothesist James Lovelock – has even greater problems. The worst-case scenario of a Chernobyl-like reactor melt-down can never be excluded, while no one has yet found a safe method of storing spent nuclear fuel which has a half-life of many thousands of years. Recently Gordon Brown announced a government plan to increase the amount of energy supplied by wind power, but this followed on the announcement of plans to expand the nuclear industry. It was hard not to see his Government as floundering with no coherent long-term energy policy because it could not disentangle all the variables.

A further complication is the fact that planning for the multitude of crises facing humanity this century needs to be co-ordinated across national and even continental boundaries. A rare example of successful worldwide co-operation was the international agreement banning CFC gases. But this didn't affect the substance of any nation's self-interest, and alternatives to CFCs were readily available. When it is a question of a ban, or a reduction, that affects a nation's self-interest across a broad range of its economic activities, agreement is much more difficult to achieve. The Kyoto Agreement on the reduction of carbon emissions is a prominent example. Few issues need to be attended to more urgently. Yet after protracted negotiations the agreement was far from a success – and not merely because of the intransigence of the United States. Many of the signatories among the industrialised nations honoured the letter rather than the spirit of the agreement, seizing on "carbon trading" as a means of having their cake and eating it. Almost all governments are concerned about the consequences of human-induced global warming, but no one wants to implement the drastic policies at home that are probably the only means of slowing, let alone reversing, the process, as the Copenhagen Climate Conference confirmed. Capitalist democracies encourage their citizens to consume, not tighten their belts.

The biological imperative that drives individuals of all species is: survive and breed. As social animals, humans achieve this partly through co-operative behaviour. But co-operation weakens the further one moves beyond the bonds of kinship, until we reach the outer edge of common humanity.

In the twentieth century, an attempt was made to establish a global organisation that took our common humanity as one of its guiding principles. The United Nations, established after World War Two, was, of course, deeply political from the start and has been used ever since by powerful nations like the USA and the former USSR to pursue their own national interests. UN agencies such as UNICEF and the World Health Organisation, however, have come as close as we have been able get to concerted and selfless action in the name of humanity. We should bear this in mind when the UN is attacked by an aggressive regime such as the one that governed the USA for the first decade of the new century. Global capitalism is diametrically opposed to the ideals of the United Nations, which explains why Bush, Cheney *et al.*

hated the organisation so much. Its existence challenged their bare-knuckle view of the world.

This is not to deny that the UN has problems, and perhaps problems that cannot be resolved under present conditions. Nonetheless, the principle behind it is the only one that can save humanity from the crises that are poised to engulf us in the next hundred years. Thinking globally, as the Green slogan has it, is in the end not enough; we need to ensure that we act globally and collectively as well – if not through the United Nations, then through some other organisation that takes the ideals on which the UN was founded and puts them into practice far more effectively.

To do this, we need to reposition our sense of common humanity, drawing it in from the periphery to the centre. This will entail a partial override of one of the strongest drives in evolutionary biology, and with it the restructuring of the global capitalist system which has appropriated that drive so successfully to its own ends. It is a question whether we can do this; yet we are an unusual species with an intelligence that is unique in the 3.6 billion-year history of life on Earth. One way or the other, the die is likely to be cast in this century.

TECHNOLOGY, GENETICS AND HAPPINESS

A distinctive feature of the technology of Early and Middle Stone Age peoples is that it did not change over vast stretches of time. It is not that innovation was absent but once an innovation had been introduced, it was reproduced with little variation across hundreds of generations and a broad geographical area. This is in complete contrast to the present, when technological change is so rapid that major developments can be counted in decades or less. In my own lifetime, for example, I have experienced the development of recorded music from wind-up gramophones and two-sided shellac 78rpm discs, to LPs, digital CDs, iPods and internet downloads.

This illustrates one of the functions of technological change in the modern world, which is to produce profusion. Collecting music on 78s was a slow process and a large collection had to be housed like a library. Today a hand-held iPod contains more music than a lifetime's collection of 78s.

It is the same with the internet. The unworldly Clerk in Chaucer's *Canterbury Tales* possessed "Twenty bookes, clad in blak or reed" that included "Aristotle and his philosophie". The number of books is mentioned because it was extremely unusual in the fourteenth century for an individual without private means to have amassed such a manuscript collection. Today, not only the works of Aristotle, but something approaching the sum of human knowledge is available to everyone at the press of a computer key.

The one feature that modern technology shares with the

technologies of the Early and Middle Stone Ages is the production of waste. The process of knapping stone to make tools resulted in a great deal of debris; the tools themselves could be retouched when they became blunt, but eventually they too were abandoned, often in substantial quantities as excavations at camp sites frequently attest. The mountains of discarded computers and monitors shipped to India and China for disposal are the twenty-first century's equivalent.

During the long periods in the Early and Middle Stone Ages when nothing changed, it might be said that hominids were in thrall to their own minds. The same tool kit was used generation after generation for thousands of years. Clearly some aspect of the mind inhibited experiment and innovation which *Homo erectus*, the Neanderthals, and early *Homo sapiens* were unable to override. Palaeoanthropologists are unsure as to the cause of this, especially in early *Homo sapiens* whose brain 150,000 years ago had the same volume and the same disposition as the brain of a modern human. One possibility is that early *Homo sapiens* lacked fully articulated speech. If this developed around 50,000 years ago, it might explain the cultural explosion that occurred at that time.

This is in direct contrast to the situation today when it could be argued that technology changes so rapidly and in such leaps that instead of it serving us, we serve technology. Such a view is counter-intuitive (though it fits with Richard Dawkins' notion of the meme). Surely it is self-evident that technological innovation is the product of human inventiveness aimed at serving human needs? The answer may be that it is only partially so.

Technology in the industrialised nations is thoroughly integrated with global capitalism, the rationale of which is the maximisation of profit. Innovation in technology may serve that purpose whether it is useful to humanity or not. The mobile phone is an example. It can be used in all kinds of emergencies and has saved lives, but this has to be set against the energy and raw materials needed for its manufacture, the energy consumed in its use, and the proliferation of hundreds of thousands of masts that are sited without regard to the environment.

Then there are the social consequences. Manufacturers'

adverts encourage the belief that it brings people together – which it does, though in what might paradoxically be described as an anti-social way. For the use of mobiles in the street and on public transport diminishes the individual's relationship with his or her surroundings, as if no one in the immediate vicinity exists. How else is it possible to have a private conversation on the phone in a crowded train, with strangers listening in?

The mobile in fact chains people together rather than uniting them. This is especially true in the world of business. It is now common on a train to sit opposite an executive who makes call after call, setting up appointments, hammering out deals, checking on subordinates back at the office. The mobile means that such people are never off duty; they are integrated, even while travelling, with the ceaseless demands of work.

More than anything, though, the mobile is the preferred medium of the bored and has produced a new form of telephone greeting: "Hello, it's only me; I'm on the train." Instead of engaging with their surroundings, many travellers – and not only the young – follow one call with another to family, or friends, or acquaintances, not because they have anything to say but because they have nothing to think about as they travel. Their eyes flicker to the screen constantly looking for text messages. Inactivity is the enemy. Mile on mile of countryside and urban landscape glide past, but they see nothing to engage with there, and rarely look out. The glow of the miniature screen, thumbs dibbing industriously at the key pad, the welcome alert of the ring tone, are what they live for during the enforced hiatus of the journey. Most people under thirty would disagree, but there is a case to be made for the mobile phone as a negative intrusion into life rather than an enhancement of it.

I suggested that we may be the servants of modern technology rather than the other way round. This is not only because the capitalist system is geared to exploit new technologies to create manufactured objects which it then tries to persuade us that we need. There is also a conjunction between human curiosity and the ultimate potential of a newly discovered technology – the pathways that may exist beyond the initial discovery, which lead scientists and technologists on and on, until every aspect has been brought to light. We believe we have control over this process; we talk about "exploiting" a technology.

Yet each new discovery is a Pandora's Box and once it is opened everything it contains pours forth. The experiments of physicists with nuclear fission in the 1930s and 40s, for example, led inexorably to the atom bomb and its successor the hydrogen bomb. This in turn led to the nuclear arms race between the USSR and the USA. Proponents of Cold War strategy argue that nuclear deterrence bought the West fifty years of peace. Yet the price was high – billions upon billions of dollars spent on armaments, thousands upon thousands of nuclear bombs and ICBMs stockpiled, that could destroy the Earth and its entire human population many times over.

It is appropriate that the acronym for this stand-off was MAD – Mutually Assured Destruction. The originators of the acronym no doubt intended the "mad" part to be one side or the other initiating a nuclear strike, knowing that retaliation would lead to their own destruction. The real madness, however, was embarking on a power struggle of this kind in the first place. The USA and the USSR might have been saved by MAD from a pre-emptive nuclear strike, one against the other, but humanity has been impoverished beyond calculation, not only by the diversion of vast funds and resources to the creation and stockpiling of the most destructive weapon ever devised, but by the fact that MAD was only effective if each side convinced the other it would launch a nuclear war if provoked. The logic of MAD hides a deep illogicality. It is the logic of *Dr Strangelove* – to save humanity we had to be prepared to destroy it.

Just as seeming logic masked the illogical in the development and deployment of nuclear weapons in the Cold War, so belief in choice masks the ways in which deep-level aspects of human nature, and the nature of modern technology, determine the "choices" scientists, technologists and politicians claim they are making.

Genetic engineering may well be the ultimate example of this. The discovery of the double helix and the mapping of the human genome are among the greatest scientific and intellectual achievements of the twentieth century. Genetics has exposed the mechanism that causes mutation within individuals of a species, the motor for variation and speciation which had eluded Darwin and his successors in the first half of the twentieth century. But it is also the greatest Pandora's Box of all since its implications for the manipulation of life on Earth are endless.

Humans have for a long time used selective breeding to improve on strains of plants and animals, as Darwin observed in *The Origin of Species*. Breeding of this kind was and is an extension of the evolutionary process, dependent on chance mutations, the difference being that favourable mutations are selected and bred for according to a teleology in the mind of the breeder.

Genetic engineering is of an entirely different order. The genetic engineer does not have to wait for a favourable mutation and then patiently breed it through several generations. A single gene can simply be taken from one species and inserted into an entirely different species to achieve a desired trait, and this may take place not only across phyla, but even across kingdoms, so that a gene that prevents blood freezing in an Arctic species of fish, for example, can be transferred to a plant. Such a transition is simply not available to the traditional breeder and it places the biotechnologist in the position of a godlike creator.

The pathways are open and are being explored. Mice have been used to grow human ears on their backs; sheep have been cloned; crops have been modified for greater yields, or to adapt them to drier or wetter conditions. There is no end to the potential. The question is, are there pathways we would not want to follow? Genetic engineering has been highly controversial from the beginning. Many people are opposed to the modification of agricultural crops, for example, and Wales has even declared itself a GM crop-free zone.

The controversy becomes intense, however, when we come to animals, especially as we approach the issue of the modification of humans. Human stem cell research has been vigorously debated in Parliament and in the press. Its supporters argue that the use of stem cells can lead to all kinds of medical advances, including cures for genetically inherited diseases that have until now proved intractable. Opponents counter – whether from religious conviction or atavistic fear of meddling with human life

– that stem cell manipulation is morally unacceptable and is the beginning of a process that will lead to "designer" babies and ultimately to human cloning – perhaps initially for couples for whom IVF and other fertility treatments have failed.

Those in favour claim that the technology need not be taken so far; that we can choose to halt genetic engineering projects at any point along a particular pathway. The history of other advanced technologies, however, suggests otherwise. Step by step, genetic engineering is advancing, producing modified crops here, quietly perfecting cloning techniques there, sizing up public receptiveness, pushing at the boundaries of the acceptable, so that the boundaries themselves begin to shift and even break down, without us hardly noticing.

These changes will be sold to us on the grounds that they increase the sum of human wellbeing and happiness. There can be no doubt that many technological developments in the twentieth century in areas such as medicine have done just that. Yet it is a question whether we have mistaken the nature of happiness, and whether in seeking it in the exploitation of advanced technologies, we have lost sight of its true source in a simple sufficiency. Such a viewpoint negates the rationale of capitalism and would undermine it if it were ever generally acknowledged.

Under present conditions, human cloning is likely to take place sometime this century. Secret experiments may already be under way, covertly encouraged by governments who condemn the process in public. The pathway exists, and no pathway in modern technology has remained unexplored, so far as I am aware, because of a consensus that it would be unwise. If it happens, humanity will have crossed what may be its last great frontier. It will be an interesting world; though interesting worlds, like "interesting times", may not be the best places in which to live.

THE COLLAPSE OF CAPITALISM?

Could the capitalist West fall as quickly and unexpectedly as the communist East did at the end of the 1980s? Until recently, this would have seemed an absurd proposal to most people. Didn't America win the Cold War? Isn't capitalist democracy the one unchallenged political and economic system across the globe? There might be theocracies and military dictatorships dotted about, but aren't they all economically backward and their people poor? There might be a growing number of thinkers and activists who oppose global capitalism, too, on environmental and ethical grounds, but what access to power do they have? We live in a world where even China, the last great bulwark of communism, has conceded that the way to prosperity is through the unleashing of capitalist enterprise in its cities.

All of this may be true. Even so, it is possible that global capitalism is nowhere near as secure as its triumphalist proponents believe. Nor perhaps is democracy which in recent years has been coupled with capitalism and sold by Bush and Blair as a universal system of government to which all peoples aspire.

Capitalism and communism were the two great wings of political thought in the nineteenth century. From the beginning they were in opposition to one another and the twentieth century became the field on which they fought for supremacy. Communism lost for a number of reasons, but underlying them is a fundamental misreading of human nature and a crude teleological view of history-as-progress with the communist state as its preordained end.

This kind of Whig interpretation is shared by capitalism. It too has a teleology that shapes historical process into a pattern of inevitability, leading to the triumph of itself. It too has a deeply flawed view of human nature which it defines in terms of our economic function, reducing us to the common denominator of "consumers".

As mentioned earlier, the biologist Niles Eldredge has suggested that individuals within a species are governed by two evolutionary imperatives, the reproductive and the economic. The one cannot be divorced from the other, for in order to reproduce, individuals have to survive by feeding themselves. It might seem that capitalism has harnessed these basic drives in a very success-ful way. Humans, too, need to eat and drink, clothe and shelter themselves, in order to survive. The urge to reproduce is also pre-eminent, as evidenced, for example, in the anguish of childless couples and the lengths they will go to have children through IVF and other fertility treatments.

Capitalism has taken these needs and processed them in hypertrophied forms. Humans are an unusual species in that sex is not limited to its reproductive function as it is in most animals; it can be, and perhaps always has been, decoupled and enjoyed for itself as one of the most powerful sensual experiences open to us. In capitalist societies sex in this sense has been appropriated and transposed to manufactured goods, fusing and confusing the one with the other. Car manufacturers, for example, do not merely advertise their products as a means of getting from one place to another, but as objects of (sexualised) desire, as in the advert in which the "supermodel" Claudia Schiffer descends the curved stairs of a chateau in her underwear, shedding items of clothing as she goes. In the final scene she steps into a car waiting on the gravelled drive, dropping her briefs out of the window with a meaningful look to camera, before driving off.

Sex now sells everything in the capitalist West, including hypertrophied versions of itself through the porno industry which has increased to vast and probably unquantifiable proportions thanks to the Internet.

The economic side of the evolutionary equation has also been hypertrophied, so that in the West we are encouraged to consume far more than is necessary for our survival. In fact modern

capitalism is predicated on making us feel the need for manufactured goods that are superfluous. In this way excess and endless
production of the new are passed off as "consumer choice",
which in itself is a sleight of hand, for the proliferation of choice
ends in the negation of real choice. What most people do in
practice is follow fashion. It is no good merely having a mobile
phone, you must have the latest model, and the models change
endlessly and rapidly. It is a system in which manufacturers, the
print media, and people-as-consumers collude. Each is looking
for the latest trend – the manufacturers because finding it before
their rivals will amass them huge profits; the media because circulation, and with it advertising revenue, depend on readers'
perception that they are getting up-to-date information on what is
being talked about; and people-as-consumers because satisfaction
is predicated on possessing manufactured (in multiple senses of
the word) objects of desire.

The problem with the capitalist view of human nature is that,
although it has understood and seized on the economic imperative that governs all species, including our own, it has done so at
the expense of other aspects of our complex being, which are
either ignored as unprofitable, or are reduced to their (sexualised)
cash value and corrupted in the process. The result is a deep
undertow of unfocussed dissatisfaction and unhappiness that
swills around in society and manifests itself in unpredictable
outbreaks of mass sentimentality and random acts of violence.
This alone is a malaise within the system which at some point will
contribute to its destruction.

As it has developed, the system is intimately linked with debt,
which, again until recently, had come to be accepted as a requirement of modern life, widely encouraged by banks and credit card
companies for whom it meant profit. Debt in the capitalist West is
what propels us into the future, allowing us to keep pace with the
latest trends as they occur. For people of my parents' generation,
debt was something to be avoided; it was a sign that you were
living beyond your means and was one step away from descent
into poverty. "Neither a borrower nor a lender be", was the
narrow precept they inherited from their own Victorian parents,
and which for the most part they contrived to live by.

The easy availability of credit has in turn made money and monetary value less real, and this has spread in ever widening circles, so that the US government under George Bush, for example, amassed overseas debts worth several trillion dollars, mostly with Chinese banks. This was the only way in which the Bush administration could pursue the ultra-capitalist policy of cutting taxes preferentially in favour of the rich while at the same time propagating hugely expensive neo-colonial wars in Iraq and Afghanistan.

The international stock market, too, deals in staggeringly large monetary exchanges which are conducted electronically so that they can appear merely notional. It is now possible to gamble millions or even billions of dollars by buying and selling on different stock markets, using the time difference of a few seconds between transactions. Huge profits can be made from small fluctuations in price, but also huge losses, and several banks were bankrupted in the 1990s by one of their own traders acting beyond the limits of his responsibility, trying to disguise a loss by ever more reckless speculation.

In fact, the whole capitalist system is beginning to appear a headlong gamble – with the Earth's finite resources, its climate and its people as the chips. For the modern capitalist, winner takes all and losers count for little. In the 1980s, Margaret Thatcher talked of the "trickle down" effect whereby the generation of wealth through largely unregulated capitalist production and speculation was supposed to increase prosperity in society at large. It did this for some social groups but the trickle was small and unevenly distributed. Preferential tax concessions, and the increasing use of off-shore banking, made the very rich a great deal richer, while the working class fragmented, leaving a substratum that was never going to pull itself out of poverty. These became, in Thatcherite terms, the undeserving poor, an underclass which had itself to blame for the condition it was in.

In Britain, this trend has been pursued by all governments since Thatcher – including the governments of Tony Blair and Gordon Brown – but they have been restrained by public support for collective institutions such as the National Health Service, which New Labour has weakened without daring to dismantle.

Where such restraints are less in evidence, as in the USA, the inadequacy of modern capitalism as a system for creating social cohesion, and maintaining a society's material infrastructure, is becoming increasingly clear – as exemplified by the federal government's response to the destruction of New Orleans by Hurricane Katrina when the most powerful nation in the world was unable to mount an effective relief operation and bodies lay rotting on the streets for days, while the President circled overhead in a plane wondering what to do.

Recovery from disasters on the scale of New Orleans cannot be left to "market forces"; response has to be immediate and it has to be co-ordinated by the government drawing on federal resources and working, preferably, to a carefully rehearsed plan. That none of this happened, or happened only days and weeks after the hurricane struck, is made worse by the fact that the danger to New Orleans from a hurricane with the right force and coming from the right direction was well known, with disaster scenarios analysed in the scientific press well before the event. *Scientific American* had predicted the results accurately in an article which explained that extensive draining of marshland around the city for building, agriculture, and other purposes, had lowered the level of the land and depleted its ability to absorb the surge of floodwater that would result from the right kind of hurricane. If nothing was done, the article concluded, the massive flooding of New Orleans was only a matter of time.

Nothing was done, of course, and the destruction of the city followed. It is the most catastrophic example to date of a problem that is fundamental to the material infrastructure of the United States. Thousands of bridges built in the 1920s and 30s are thought to be unsafe; reservoirs built during the same period are silting up; water reserves in the West, including the great Ogallala aquifer that stretches from Nebraska to Texas, are being drained at an unsustainable rate – yet there appear to be no plans for restricting building or population movement, or indeed water use, in the affected states, or to co-ordinate, for example, the examination and repair of bridges on a federal basis.

Suddenly, in the twenty-first century, America has come to seem less powerful than it was. Its armed forces, geared to fight a titanic global war with the former USSR, struggles to contain guerilla fighters armed with small arms, improvised mines, and deploying suicide bombers, in Iraq and Afghanistan. At home, it cannot mount an effective rescue and recovery operation in response to natural disaster. Geologically, North America is a very dynamic continent. A massive earthquake along the line of the San Andreas fault in densely populated California is only a matter of time. Nobody knows what the vast magma chamber that lies beneath Yellowstone National Park is going to do. Were it to erupt, as some geologists are predicting, it would cause devastation on a scale that would be unprecedented in human history. It may be that neither of these events will happen in the course of the next thousand years; what Hurricane Katrina revealed, however, is the ineffectiveness of the minimal government favoured by neo-capitalism in dealing with natural disasters on any significant scale.

Capitalist democracy fails human beings at a more immediate and personal level too. In the United States, a substantial percentage of the population work at jobs that are so badly paid that they have to take on a second job. Unionisation is discouraged so that workers employed by giant retail companies like Wall-Mart have no organised means of representing their own interests as against those of the company. In states like Mississippi, poverty in the rural black community rivals that in countries like Guyana, the second poorest nation in the Caribbean after Haiti.

It does not have to be like this. As the New Deal showed in the 1930s, government intervention can do much to alleviate poverty and redistribute wealth, but such *dirgisme* has been anathema to the proponents of minimalist government who have dominated politics in America and Britain during the past thirty years, arguing that as much as possible should be left to the market which will "adjust" as conditions change. Moreover, the immoderate wealth of multinationals and of individuals in areas like stockbroking is a public good because it generates prosperity lower down the economic chain. These arguments are patently false, yet for thirty years they have remained unchallenged in mainstream politics in America and Britain, and throughout most of Europe as well.

Then came October 2008, when the world was plunged into its greatest financial crisis since 1929. As major banks went under in the United States and Britain; as stock markets fell and fell; as investors, from individual speculators to county councils, saw their investments wiped out overnight; as it seemed that ordinary depositors might lose their life savings, and Iceland effectively declared itself bankrupt, it was unclear for several months whether or not an unstoppable cascade had been set in motion that would destroy the financial system on which global capitalism depends. Losses were counted not in millions but in hundreds of billions of dollars, and government after government was forced to intervene, guaranteeing the banks with many more billions of public money, effectively nationalising them against the deepest convictions of neo-capitalism, in a desperate attempt to avert the total collapse of the system.

Influential voices, including George Soros and Warren Buffet, had warned for some years that the global financial market was unstable, and that a crisis of this sort was a matter of time. They were unheeded, however, because for a generation governments in the United States and Britain had bought into the Reaganite-Thatcherite ideology that the market knows best, and that it should be left to regulate itself with a minimum of government interference. The events of September and October 2008 showed in the clearest way that this was not true. Reagan and Thatcher had blinded themselves to the fact that, when faced with the opportunity to amass inconceivable wealth, all too many people will take it, even if this means putting at risk the livelihood of millions. It is an irony that the ideologues of a capitalist system based on the manipulation of acquisitiveness, failed to see that deregulating the banks and the stock market could only lead to disaster. Faith in the ideology was complete, and anyone who suggested that a mixed economy, for example, might be more stable was derided. The future was already here, and unrestricted avarice (in an inversion of values that has become the norm) was the highest good.

As a result of prompt dirigiste action by governments, a total collapse of the financial system seems to have been averted. Even with closer government regulation, however, and a more

chastened attitude (for now) on the part of financiers and speculators, the fundamental principles of the global capitalist system
remain in place. Small government and a powerful, independent
business section are still considered by many to be the only way
to prosperity, not just for ourselves, but for all the peoples of the
world. Despite the profound shock of the crisis – and despite the
phenomenon of Barack Obama – the system is therefore likely to
remain as inherently unstable and unsustainable as it was before.

In retrospect, the crisis of 2008-09 was a severe tremor which
the capitalist democracies were able to withstand. We have,
nonetheless, built our system on a subduction zone, and there will
be worse earthquakes to come. If another violent oscillation in the
financial system coincides, for example, with the failure of the
harvest in the North American grain belt (perhaps as a result of
the adverse effects of global warming), or with peak oil, or a full-
scale pandemic, the outcome may be very different next time.

WHAT THE RAVEN TOLD THE EAGLE

Reading about climate change in the press, you could be forgiven for thinking that nature is normally in a state of equilibrium which humankind has unbalanced through its reckless discharge of greenhouse gases into the atmosphere. This is about as far from the truth as it is possible to get. Thanks largely to plate tectonics, nature has been in a state of flux for thousands of millions of years. Antarctica, covered by an ice sheet for the past 25 million years, had a sub-tropical climate and a flora and fauna to match before the Antarctic plate drifted onto the South Pole. A mere 20,000 years ago during the last ice age, Britain was linked by a land bridge to Continental Europe that stretched south in a line from the Wash to southern Jutland, forming a harsh tundra plain. At the same time, an ice sheet covered what is now the northern states of the USA from Iowa to New York. In places, according to Niles Eldredge, it was three kilometres thick. That ice age ended some 10,000 years ago, since when the Northern Hemisphere has experienced a mild interglacial climate which allowed human civilisations to flourish and expand. If past oscillations are anything to go by, the Northern Hemisphere ought to experience a new ice age within the next couple of thousand years which would have as catastrophic an impact on humanity's future as the current period of global warming is likely to do. In the vast stretches of geological time, ecological systems chase each other like cloud shadow over the hills.

But we can only conceive of the Earth like this through an act of what might be called intellectual imagination. We have not evolved to think on such timescales. For us, experiential time covers at most five generations, those of our grandparents, our parents, ourselves, our children and grandchildren, a hundred years or so – a period so short that it cannot be measured by geological time where datings of plus or minus half a million years are considered good by geologists. We live in the here and now. Go back even a mere five or six thousand years and you are beyond Ancient History in a world that can only be glimpsed through its fragmentary artefacts and bones.

It is not surprising therefore that most of us think of nature as comprising the birds and plants, animals and insects, with which we have grown up. The seasonal migration of swallows and martins, the succession of wayside flowers in summer, crane flies and moths at the window panes in autumn, these are what we know through the senses, giving us an illusion of timelessness through what appear to be enduring cycles. And this is reinforced in poetry and art. When you open a fourteenth century illuminated manuscript and see in its margins the marvellously animated paintings of goldfinches and bullfinches, you know that the anonymous artist saw what you see and took the same delight in these beautiful birds. Our sense of nature unites us across the generations, becoming one of the guarantors of a common humanity.

Recently, however, this tradition has been challenged by profound demographic and cultural changes and by the rapid destruction of the Holocene ecosystems to which we belong. These developments have taken place in tandem and are global in scale.

The drift from the land that began in Europe in the nineteenth century as its nations industrialised has now become a stampede as people crowd into the expanding megacities of Asia and Central and South America. This has been paralleled by technological developments, most notably television, IT and the World Wide Web, which have helped create an urban mentality even in rural areas of heavily populated countries like Wales and England. The walkman, the iPod, the mobile phone have added to the mix, so that increasingly experience is mediated electronically rather than through direct sensory perception of the world around us. Nature does not have much to say to this emergent culture where, in so far as literature is relevant at all, the preference is for urban *noir* that celebrates the life of the city's tenements and streets.

In this context, nature poetry fares badly. The term can hardly be used without quotation marks, suggesting its irrelevance to the self-referential city of the mind where most of us now live. We are in the process of crossing a threshold, one of three or four in human evolutionary history, which is likely to have consequences as profound as the shift from hunter-gathering to agriculture eight to four thousand years ago. It is not possible to discern all the consequences, but they are likely to include the further marginal-isation of nature in our culture and the effective rejection of the tradition of poetry that celebrates our complex relation to it.

This tradition has existed for at least fifteen hundred years in Europe, during which time nature has been an integral part of the poetic consciousness, not necessarily in the form of nature poetry (which is essentially a Romantic and Post-Romantic develop-ment) but as nature *in* poetry, a protean source of imagery and symbol, and a yardstick with which to measure our humanity. It is there, for example, in heroic verse. "He was food for ravens, he was benefit to the crow," says the narrator of *Y Gododdin* (in A.O.H. Jarman's translation) about a fallen Welsh warrior. Two hundred or so years later in the Old English poem *Beowulf*, a messenger foresees the battle which will annihilate Beowulf's people after his death:

>   …the black raven
> eager over the doomed   speaks of many things
> tells the eagle   how he fared at the feast
> while with the wolf   he plundered the slain.

Ravens, eagles, wolves scavenging a battlefield would have been a familiar sight in the Iron Age. In the stylised poetry of the period they became symbols of the hero's worth. The *Gododdin* warriors were not cowards, the crows and ravens proclaim; they chose death rather than dishonour. If extinction is the fate of Beowulf's tribe, they too will face it open-eyed.

Nature in poetry has continued into modern times. It is characteristic of Dylan Thomas, for example, who is not a nature poet at all, though his poems are freighted with images drawn from nature:

> It was my thirtieth year to heaven
> Woke to my hearing from harbour and neighbour wood
> And the mussel pooled and the heron
> Priested shore....

So begins "Poem in October". As it unfolds, water-birds, herons again, larks, blackbirds, owls, apples, pears, red currents, fish, trees tumble over each other exuberantly as he both celebrates his birthday and laments an irretrievably lost past. The images are drawn from Thomas's experience of rural west Wales, but like the beasts of battle they are transformed into symbols for a particular set of human circumstances and emotions.

Are we part of nature or separate from it? Our genus, *Homo*, certainly evolved through speciation, from *Homo habilis* who lived two million years BP, down to ourselves. Ancestor species and collateral branches like the Neanderthals inhabited ecological niches indistinguishable from other species in the Pleistocene, with the exception of their emergent use of tools, which in the hands of *Homo sapiens* led within a brief 50,000 years to the megacities and hi-technology civilisation of today. Perhaps, as a result of this huge cultural shift, we should think of ourselves as both part of nature and apart from it at the same time; by turns fascinated and appalled at our strange duality; sometimes turning toward nature, as in the Romantic period, and sometimes turning away, as in the megacities of our own age.

This duality has been a persistent theme in Post-Romantic, Post-Darwinian poetry. The sense of nature's otherness, for example, is finely caught in Thomas Hardy's "The Fallow Deer at the Lonely House":

> One without looks in to-night
>   Through the curtain-chink
> From the sheet of glistening white;
> One without looks in to-night

> As we sit and think
> By the fender-brink.

The humans are distanced from the deer by their minds, by the capacity for thought of a kind which produced such cultural constructs as the house and the protective warmth of its fire. The people of the house are turned in on themselves; the deer is forever apart in the cold winter world:

> We do not discern those eyes
>   Watching in the snow;
> Lit by lamps of rosy dyes
> We do not discern those eyes
>   Wondering, aglow,
>   Fourfooted, tiptoe.

Poetry in this tradition oscillates between the human and the natural, using one to measure the other. In "The Owl", after a long day's walk, Edward Thomas enters an inn, looking forward to food and warmth. The night is shut out, except for the persistent cry of an owl, "Shaken out long and clear upon the hill". The call of the wild bird at home in the darkness serves again as a measure of the distance between humans and nature. The poet is lucky in the safety and comfort of the inn, a constructed human world, to be excluded from which brings only misery:

> And salted was my food, and my repose,
> Salted and sobered, too, by the bird's voice
> Speaking for all who lay under the stars,
> Soldiers and poor, unable to rejoice.

The owl "speaks" through the poet's imagination here, though Edward Thomas would have been aware that this is a conceit, a device to reflect nature back on the human. For poets after Darwin, nature "speaks" only to itself, as in Hilary Llywellyn-Williams's poem "Asking the Bees". Listening to the hum of bees among flowers

> *Tell me* I whisper

Into the honeyed clamour
What is the news this summer?

The bees' "conversation" however is self-referential; humanity and its questions are forever an irrelevance:

Will the sun bless us
will my wish be granted
where does this way lead?

she insists.

But the bees' predictions
are all of the colours of flowers

their weight and sweetness
and the shortening days.

If we can no longer charm the birds and animals like Orpheus, we nonetheless still feel a need to interact with them, to entwine their lives with ours. In "The Goldcrest", Anna Wigley describes taking in one of the tiny birds that is in shock,

his thin stiffened feet turned up
like a dying man's hands above the sheet.

The image is a drastic one, comparing the minuscule goldcrest ("In the palm he was light as a leaf,/a bare ounce of barely-beating life") with the huge, to the bird, hands of a human. The image unbalances us because it is so unexpected and makes us look more closely, but it also affirms the common bond between all living things in the face of suffering and death (the bird in this case survives) and the ways in which the human mind can empathise with life that is so different from our own.

In one of Ted Hughes's finest nature poems, "Swifts", he too plunders the human to describe the birds, through images reproduced in a series of quick-sketch notes as he scrambles to set down their reckless, exuberant flight:

> And here they are, here they are again
> Erupting across yard stones
> Shrapnel-scatter terror. Frog-gapers,
> Speedway goggles, international mobsters....

The poem celebrates the birds' return each spring and the sense of continuity they bring for humans:

> They've made it again,
> Which means the globe's still working, the Creation's
> Still waking refreshed, our summer's
> Still all to come....

This urge to find renewal in nature and what can only be called joy is very strong in humans. In "Two Pewits", Edward Thomas watches a pair of lapwings as they swirl in the dusk of a spring evening,

> More white than is the moon on high
> Riding the dark surge silently;
> More black than earth....

The imagery evokes precisely the eerie quality of these birds in their last flight before settling to roost. (I once saw several hundred lining the furrows of a ploughed field, their white bellies gleaming in the dark as if they attracted and concentrated every last vestige of light.) To Thomas, their flight is exhilarating as he stands there watching; the birds themselves seeming released almost from the bonds of the earth:

> And merrily they cry
> To the mischievous Spring sky,
> Plunging earthward, tossing high,
> Over the ghost who wonders why
> So merrily they cry and fly,
> Nor choose 'twixt earth and sky,
> While the moon's quarter silently
> Rides, and earth rests as silently.

Edward Thomas wrote in the confidence that nature as he

knew it would always be there, a deep resource of images and themes which readers would respond to because a variety of birds and animals and plants were a familiar part of their world. When he wrote of the lapwings they were a common sight over arable farm land, as they were in my childhood in the 1940s and 50s. But this is no longer so. In Wales alone, the population of breeding lapwings has fallen by 70 percent in the past 20 years, and in most parts of the country they are now absent or rare. The lapwing has been added to the Amber List along with many other species. It is not that "Two Pewits" cannot be appreciated if you haven't seen the bird, but the poem is predicated on the assumption that you have and that images from your own memory will interact with and illuminate the images on the page. Reading "Two Pewits" is a two-way process.

A century on and no poet can make Edward Thomas's assumption or share his confidence, and not just because a few once familiar species are becoming rare or disappearing altogether. Not just because of the wide reach of the city of the mind, either, that turns away from nature to gaze in a hi-technology mirror. Nature itself is changing profoundly and becoming unfamiliar to us in the process, as the sixth mass extinction of species in the history of life on Earth gets under way.

During the greatest mass extinction at the Permo-Triassic boundary 180 million years ago, some 95 percent of species became extinct. Predictions for the current extinction, which are necessarily uncertain, suggest that species loss will be between 35 and 65 percent over the next few hundred years. The effects of this are likely to have serious consequences for humans, for each mass extinction creates a bottleneck and it is a lottery as to which species squeeze through. It is certainly not necessarily the "fittest", and for all our cleverness, there is no guarantee that *Homo sapiens* will be among the survivors.

We live in the here and now, and again it takes an act of the intellectual imagination to think on this time scale and in these terms. Even so, our faith in the stability of nature has been seriously eroded. A tornado hits the village of Bow Street in Ceredigion, a month's rain falls in a single day in June and flash floods cause havoc in northern England. Just extreme weather of a kind that has always existed? Or a sign of a new instability in the climate which we will have to get used to? Birds nest earlier each spring, patterns of migration are changing, exotic species penetrate our skies and coastal waters; once common songbirds become rarities and fall away from human memory.

How should the poet, for whom nature is an imaginative resource, respond? The common bond of experience between the poet and the reader, mediated through the nature poem, can no longer be relied on. Soon we will need editors' notes on the behaviour of the lapwing; a selection of John Clare's poetry already has photographs of flowers and animals to help the reader visualise what the poems describe.

The natural world of the Holocene, the past 10,000 years, always was provisional, though on our limited time scale it did not seem so. That illusion has been shattered for good. It is tempting to turn to the elegiac, to lament the passing of what poetry has celebrated for generations, and there is a place for this. However, we are poised on one of the great thresholds of human consciousness, and of the nature that until now sustained us. It is highly unlikely that we will be able to unite as a species in order to solve the problem of global warming and its ultimate cause, human overpopulation. It is even more unlikely, given these pressures, that we will be able to bring to a halt the current mass extinction of species. Despite our ingenuity, the scale of the problems we face are too great and too complex for our brains.

Under these circumstances, the nature poet should be an explorer of, it may be, new possibilities or, it may be, a human and natural tragedy – but certainly of a very different world from the one humanity has known for so long. For whatever emerges in the next decades and centuries, we cannot go back, we can only go on, and we will need a new poetry to interpret what is happening and what we will have become.

YNYS LAS

Ynys Las, just North of Aberystwyth, is a five kilometre stretch of sand separated from an area of dunes by a natural shingle bank. At its northernmost point it ends in the estuary of the Dyfi; to the South it merges into Borth beach with its protective sea wall and long line of wooden breakwaters.

To walk there at low tide is to experience large vistas of sky and far horizons, the sea booming with the fall on fall of waves that rush across the sand then seep and ebb away, leaving the lace of their foam. The prevailing winds are onshore westerlies enabling you to see what weather is coming. Banks of white cloud may stay far out on the horizon all morning, leaving the shore bright with sunlight; or a steep wall of darkness may build up, with curtains of rain that appear to sway slowly over the water, though you know they are approaching rapidly. Soon enough, the headland at the South end of Borth is enveloped and obscured, and then the rain overwhelms the shore, hissing on the sea and pitting the sand. Caught out, there is nowhere to shelter and you are in for a soaking. If the rain turns to hail, it is driven by the wind into a stinging assault on your face and hands, making you vulnerable, no longer an interested observer but a reluctant participant in nature's large-scale systems over which you have no control.

I go there mostly to watch birds. Even in poor weather there is something to see – cormorants on the spit of sand near the fast flowing mouth of the Dyfi, holding out wings like ragged scarecrows; lesser black-backed gulls with their smart black-and-white plumage, in mixed flocks with herring gulls that look washed-out by contrast; oystercatchers following their orange beaks in low rapid flight over the waves; stonechats and wheatears in the dunes. And there is always the excitement of what might turn up, especially during the spring and autumn migrations when there can be large flocks of waders – dunlin, sanderling, curlew; and once in May three hundred bar-tailed godwits in their magnificent rufous breeding plumage. Sometimes gannets cruise the coast from the South, a hundred or more circling and diving in the waves if they locate a shoal of fish, their black-and-white wings shining in the sun as they rise and bank, then plunge to spear the water again and again. There are also true exotics, like the little egret I saw fishing in a tidal sand pool, its long white crest blowing in an onshore wind, its body balanced over grey legs and incongruous citrus-yellow feet. A southern European species, it has been extending its range northward for some years; it is a regular now in the saltings at nearby Traeth Maelgwyn. Before the days of the tourist, the dunes must have been a substantial breeding site for ground-nesting birds; even today a small colony of ringed plovers has its nests there, almost invisible among the sand and stones.

In the early morning there are few people at Ynys Las – occasional dog owners letting their dogs leap and bark at the sea; a rider whose horse canters through spent waves along the tideline. Almost none of these, you can tell, are interested in the birds, the dog owners letting their animals chase and disturb the flocks of gulls and waders as they stroll along, nature for them being a human pleasure ground, the birds small details in a broader scene. Occasionally there is a woman photographer who crouches with a telephoto lens, taking images of the birds, but she is rare. It is possible to avoid people at Ynys Las when the tide is out, passing them at a distance with a nod.

Birds are not the only interest on the long shoreline. Wherever you look there is something to see, and walking the sands the eye constantly adjusts to scale and distance. Under your feet the beach is littered with the shells of spiny cockles, mussel and razor shells, oyster shells and the large cupped shells of *Arctis islandica*, many of the latter still with their coating of black protein, though this soon gets abraded by the waves. After a storm stranger creatures can be driven ashore – goose barnacles that attach themselves in thick colonies to the undersides of driftwood and are usually found far out to sea. Suspended on fleshy stalks, they open delicate pearl-grey shells to feed. One colony on the rope of what might have been a yacht's painter was still alive when I found it, the creatures flinching on their stalks when I touched them. Days later they were further along the beach, thrown up on the shingle embankment, the stalks rubbery and gelatinous and the barnacles dead. I tore some off their mooring and took them home, leaving the bodies to rot in the garden for the shells.

Scattered along the sand there are dead crabs too, that dangle their pink, armoured legs if you pick them up, and the remains of seabirds – herring gulls and once a guillemot – that look like crash victims on the long wet vistas.

Tighten the focus as you walk toward the Dyfi and you begin to pick out nuts and seeds that have been deposited at the tide line. Hazel nuts, acorns, beech mast, they are mostly from northern European trees, but there is always the chance of something unfamiliar, floated across the Atlantic on the Gulf Stream and by the prevailing westerly winds. Anything unusual can be planted in a pot to see if it will germinate after its long passage over the ocean, performing in miniature one of Darwin's experiments.

When wind-driven rain closes in and a fine spray from the waves is blown across the shore, Borth, and Aberdyfi across the mouth of the estuary, disappear from view and it can seem as if you are the last human, trudging across the bare sands. Then the detritus deposited by storms makes you a forlorn Crusoe surrounded by the rubbish of a failed civilisation. Balks of timber, empty oil drums and chemical drums, wooden crates, milk cartons, bottles, wellington boots, beer cans, nylon ropes, come and go with the tide. Above all there is plastic – bottles, bags, milk crates, equipment from ships – much of it unidentifiable as it breaks up and lodges in the pebble bank. It is identifiable as plastic, though, by the bright crudeness of its colours. Scientists have discovered that there is not a shoreline in the world unpolluted by plastic; even the finest sandy beach is impregnated with tiny grains as the artefacts of our world are ground down by the waves. In the Pacific there is an area the size of the United States that is a soup of thrown-away plastic.

At Ynys Las you are dwarfed for a while by the scale of the

forces that shape our planet, weather systems that rise and swirl overhead, tides that sweep in and out endlessly, fast currents that can make swimming dangerous; a world that is shifting and provisional yet which forms a grand, unified whole. With the exception, that is, of ourselves – the intelligent species, the one that perhaps should have been designated *Homo faber* by Linnaeus, because we are above all the makers, whose ingenuity we once believed would bring nature to our heel.

It is a vision that is losing its hold, though, as we teeter from crisis to crisis, as the negative impact of humans on nature becomes ever clearer. For the idea of progress that has guided the West since the Enlightenment is beginning to look battered and flawed. Unintended consequences, some of which have lain dormant or disguised for a long time, are beginning to disturb us with their scale and complexity. Perhaps more even than *Homo faber*, we are *Homo destructor*, subject to ripples of panic as we come to realise, obscurely, how small we are, yet averting our eyes as best we can because we do not really want to change the way we live. Perhaps, some say, the science is wrong; perhaps, some hope, the politicians and technologists will know what to do.

There can be no doubt, however, that humanity and the Earth have gone beyond a point of no return as a direct result of the impact of humans on the Earth's natural processes, and that the next fifty years will see upheavals of a kind that may make the twentieth century seem, for all its barbarity, a golden age. As the bus weaves through a country lane on the way from Borth to my home in Comins Coch, the familiarity of the fields of sheep, the hedgerows, the farms and villages, the normality of people's lives as they get on and off the bus, make such thoughts seem unreal and unduly pessimistic. This is to ignore the reports that are being filed now day after day about species loss, pollution, desertification, global warming and the rapid retreat of polar and glacial ice. My sense of being an observer at Ynys Las is what is wrong; for whether we like it or not, admit it or not, we are participants in the Earth's dynamic processes – and likely soon to be put in our place by the immensity of the geophysical and biological disruptions we have set in motion.

CANTRE'R GWAELOD

According to legend, what is now Cardigan Bay was once a prosperous kingdom ruled by Gwyddno Garanhir. Known as Cantre'r Gwaelod, the Lowland Hundred, it contained sixteen cities, its land defended from the sea by a series of embankments and dikes. The keeper of the defences was Seithenyn. After a night of drinking, Seithenyn failed to close the sluices and the sea inundated Cantre'r Gwaelod, drowning everyone except the king. On a quiet evening it is said the bells of the cities' churches can be heard tolling far out beneath the water.

The reality is different yet in its way more fascinating. At the end of the last Ice Age dry land stretched fourteen miles and more out into what is now Cardigan Bay. According to David B. James, in *Ceredigion: Its Natural History*, a salt marsh developed above a bed of clay in the area as the climate grew milder. Over time the salinity of the marsh decreased and fresh water plants became dominant. At some point, a lowering of the water table allowed northern latitude trees – birch, Scots pine, and later oak – to establish themselves. Their hold on the lowland was temporary, however. Five hundred to a thousand years on, by David James's estimate, water levels rose again and the forest was drowned in perhaps two to three feet of water. Marsh conditions were re-established and tree stumps and fallen trunks were preserved in the anaerobic conditions of a shallow peat bog.

Again according to David James, radiocarbon dating places the Scots pine forest at 5600-6000 years BP, while the oaks are later, perhaps 4000-4800 years BP. When conditions are right, stumps of trees and even whole trunks can be seen at low tide at

Ynys Las, Borth, Clarach, and Tan-y-bwlch. The trunks are aligned in a South-West to North-East direction, with what would have been the crowns of the trees pointing South-West. It is possible they were blown down during a violent gale. Often there is no sign of the remains of the forest; strong currents and the tides have covered them with sand. After a storm, though, the beach at the north end of Borth can be littered with the stumps of pines, the wood surprisingly soft to the touch and slimy with algae. The shattered, blackened stumps and their twisted roots look like decayed molars in an ancient mouth.

The forest, or succession of forests, drowned when sea levels rose as a result of the great glacial melt at the end of the last Ice Age. The stumps and prone trunks that can be seen today are all that is left of the land that gave rise to the legend of Cantre'r Gwaelod.

The legend itself, with its sixteen cities and elaborate sea defences, is a medieval accretion. It must be based, though, on folk memory stretching back to the Mesolithic. Certain striking geological features in the area would have encouraged the legend. On the beach at Wallog, between Clarach and Borth, there is an extraordinary structure, Sarn Cynfelin, which stretches like a causeway out into the sea. It extends, according to David James, for twelve kilometres under the water. The sarn is so straight, so perfectly constructed, that it is almost impossible not to believe that it is man-made. In fact it consists of glacial debris and is the remains of a medial moraine exposed as the glacier retreated at the end of the last Ice Age. It is easy to see how such an impressive structure came to be viewed as a causeway, or part of the elaborate sea defences of the legendary Cantref.

Five thousand eight hundred years ago, when the birch and Scots pine forest was well established, "Cantre'r Gwaelod" must have been a pleasant place. It would have been filled with animal and bird life. Red deer were certainly there because antlers have on rare occasions been cast up by the sea; but there are likely to have been beavers, too, as well as wild boar, bears, wolves and foxes, and a wide variety of bird life common to northern woods.

Mesolithic hunters certainly wandered there. Near the entrance to Aberystwyth harbour there is an unassuming mound on which a concrete pillbox was built during the Second World War. Known as Pen Hukin, it is a Mesolithic tool workshop producing, among other stone implements, tiny microliths that are characteristic of the culture. Working there, it would have been possible to look out over the shelving plain to the West with its forests and lakes and remnants of marsh. Golden eagles and perhaps sea eagles would have soared above the canopy.

Human memory and oral tradition can preserve events, names, and lineages over long periods of time even if they become distorted through constant retelling. I have often wondered if "monsters" like Grendel in the Old English heroic poem *Beowulf* are not in fact folk memories – hypertrophied beyond recognition – of the last of the Neanderthals who died out in Western Europe some 30,000 years ago. No memory appears to have survived, however, of the hunter-gatherers who roamed the forest of Cantre'r Gwaelod. What were their tribes? What language did they speak? (Not Welsh, certainly.) What names did they give one another? Where did they go when the sea level rose, overwhelming their world? There is no way of knowing. Such knowledge is lost to us forever.

Today we build our lives on a new frontier between land and sea. At Aberystwyth and Borth sea walls protect us from spring tides and westerly storms. From Borth to Ynys Las a golf course trails its ribbon of fairways and greens either side of a road so straight it could have been built by the Romans. It is very un-Welsh. Not so the ribbon development of houses, the caravan park, the drained marsh with bleak wire fencing and bedraggled sheep.

There is a permanent air of impermanence. In winter the caravan park at Borth is empty and half the shops are closed. In summer tourists come and go, wandering along the sea wall, not seeming to know what to do. There is a sense of slowness, of taking one's time. Every hour a green-and-white Arriva bus lumbers though the long main street then out to Ynys Las Turn where it waits in the silence, passed now and then by a car or pick-up truck, before heading back to Aberystwyth with its few passengers.

The provisional nature of it all has a kind of honesty. Looking out over the drained pasture to the pale shapes of the Cambrian Mountains in the East and the mountains of Gwynedd in the North; watching the tide back up into the Dyfi estuary until it becomes a glittering inland lake; or crossing the dunes to the sand-strewn road that would soon be buried if left to itself, you cannot evade the triumph of time, its arrow hurtling into the future, obliterating everything in its wake.

The morning after a storm is a good time to walk the five kilometres of sand between Borth and Ynys Las. Large slabs of peat laid down seven or eight thousand years ago in the vanished marshes of Cantre'r Gwaelod can be flung up on the beach, only to be snatched back by the next high tide and swirled again under the waters of the Bay. Most of the remains of Scots pine on the shore seem to be from young trees judging by the diameter of their trunks; but sometimes the roots and shattered base of a much larger and older tree will be exposed, its powerful root system disappearing under the beach. It is massive, immovable. Yet it too is soon dragged back into its sand and salt-water tomb.

Sea levels will rise this century though nobody knows by how much. In Ceredigion there will be a new negotiation between the land and the Bay. Borth may have to be abandoned, the cost of sea defences being prohibitive for such a small community. Then the large expanse of drained flatland will become a sea marsh again, and the dunes at Ynys Las will be clawed back under the waves. There will be few new bells to add to the ones tolling in the cities of Cantre'r Gwaelod, however. The legend was the product of an age when Wales was Roman Catholic. Chapels rarely have bells and most have in any case been converted to secular use. For some time, though, Borth's sea wall will be a marker in the Bay, visible at low tide, its presence indicated by white breakers at high tide, especially in stormy weather – a good location for in-shore fishermen, perhaps, if there are still humans in the area.

The erosive power of water is extraordinary. For thirty-five years I have visited a small village in North-west Jutland. When I first went there a concrete bunker built by the German occupiers in the Second World War faced out to sea, perched well inland on the sandy soil. Little by little, however, the land was eroded and year by year the sea came closer to the bunker. Then one year the concrete structure was lapped by water at high tide. Soon it was in the sea itself. For a while you could see its flat roof dunking in the waves. Then it was gone. If you had diving gear I suppose you could find it today, an artificial reef in miniature where seaweeds have gained a purchase, home perhaps to crustacea, bivalves like the mussel, starfish, sea urchins and fish; perhaps a conger eel has made its home in the darkness of the interior, ready to strike through the bunker's narrow, slitted aperture. For the rest, standing on the shoreline today, you could not guess that it had ever existed.

REMEMBERING BIRDS

When I was very small, perhaps three or four years old, and so toward the end of the Second World War, someone gave me a *Book of Garden Birds*, one of those children's books of the period with thick, almost cardboard, pages. Each page had brightly coloured paintings of blue tits and great tits, chaffinches and bullfinches, robins and blackbirds, with the text in a large font size that weaved itself around the paintings. Or at least I think it did; almost certainly I couldn't read at the time and so the words were a dense mass of meaningless symbols that I took little notice of. The paintings were different. I don't recall being aware of birds before that gift, but I remember sitting by the fire with the book open on my knees – so it might have been a Christmas present – absorbed in the birds' plumage, their forms, their blackberry eyes, the dynamics of them as they perched confidently on a branch or flew across the white space of a page.

I am sure that it was after this that I began to look at birds through the kitchen window as they fought for scraps in the yard and tried to stalk them in summer in the garden hedge. A few years later, when I started to get pocket money, I bought other books about birds, which I still have – *Eggs and Nests of British Birds*, *Nests and Eggs*, *A Pocket Book of British Birds' Eggs and Nests*, the titles indicating that around 1952 or 1953 I had turned my attention to egg collecting. My cousin Alan had given me his small collection that included a magnificent curlew's egg taken from a nest on the Mardy, and I had been stirred by my mother's tales of the collection amassed by her brother, my Uncle Ron, in the Forest of Dean. We rarely went to visit him, so I had to imagine the collection. It had, she said, the eggs of almost every bird in the British Isles, including that rarity of rarities, a hummingbird's egg, which he had extricated with tweezers from its nest, lodged in a tiny hole in a wall. The Forest of Dean, I decided, must be an extraordinary place. Not till a few years later, when I had obtained T.A. Coward's *The Birds of the British Isles* in three volumes, did I realise that the hummingbird could not be. Later still, hearing more of my Uncle's exploits as filtered through my mother – all of them improbable and told with deep serious-ness – I realised that I had been introduced to the tall tale, and that Uncle Ron would have bedded down well in Yoknapatawpha County.

Yet the tale of the hummingbird's egg has stayed with me as if it were something true. I can see a moss-covered wall in the Forest and a crouching figure, and a hand inserting silver tweezers into the crevice, then delicately, slowly, drawing it back with the prize of an egg. I was at an age when I believed what my mother said (she herself believed the story when she told it me) and I imagined it so intensely that the tale has the quality of remem-bered experience, as if I had been there at my Uncle's side and shared his thrill at such a find.

I was never a successful egg collector myself. I always felt an element of guilt when I discovered a nest in a hedgerow and felt squeamish at the process of piercing an egg at each end then blowing out what you hoped would be yoke, not the bloodied foetus of a bird. So my collection didn't grow much, and when, as I was peering into a hedge on the Old Hereford Road, a man on a bicycle stopped and said "You're not bird nesting, are you?" to which I answered "No", I gave up. Later of course I came to realise how damaging egg collecting was to bird populations, but in the late 1940s and early 1950s almost every boy did it because that is what you did, just as we all wore a knife with at least a four-inch blade, hanging in a sheath from our belts.

I never look for nests now, but the sight of a mottled or sky-blue egg shell broken and discarded on the ground from which the bird has hatched, reanimates the excitement I felt when I was twelve or thirteen on parting a hedge to see a clutch of eggs with their perfect oval shapes and rare colour and markings. I always have to stop and pick the shell up and examine it carefully before walking on.

Just as I can remember the exact location in the Forest of Dean where Uncle Ron discovered the hummingbird's egg – in my mind the wall is very old, about five feet tall, situated under a stand of beech trees, dappled light filtering down to brush the lichened stones – so I am able to recall precisely where I *did* see birds of different species for the first time, with an intensity and precision that eclipses almost every other kind of memory.

Perhaps it has something to do with the sudden and unexpected nature of so many of these encounters – the neon-blue flash of a kingfisher breaking cover on the banks of the River Usk; or the undulating flight of a green woodpecker on the wooded slopes of the Deri; a glimpse that can be recalled at will, more real than any photograph or nature film.

Some encounters, though, are bizarre in ways that make them seem like the imagined memory of the hummingbird's egg. One day in summer when I was perhaps eleven or twelve, I was lying on my stomach on the banks of the Usk at a place where the river curved, bringing deep water up close, undercutting the rich red soil of the bank. I don't think I was looking for anything in particular, but suddenly there below me, two or three feet under the swiftly flowing water, was a bird walking on the bottom, its head darting left and right as it made its way upstream. I had no idea what it was, or that a bird could do such a thing, pacing there as if an underwater life was its element. Consulting T.A. Coward at home, I realised that it was a dipper and that these birds of the fast flowing rivers and streams of Wales do this regularly in search of food. Although I have often watched dippers since, bobbing with their white bibs on stones in the glitter of the Usk's shallows, I have never again seen one foraging underwater, and I sometimes question whether the memory is real.

There is something of the process of writing poetry in these encounters. Often you go out to a promising location and see nothing, or at any rate nothing unusual; then when you have given up and turned for home, the unexpected happens and you are presented with a gift, the perfection of a bird that appears as if just for you. You could not have arranged the moment, and it will never happen in the same way again. Like the time in Saskatchewan when an acquaintance took me birdwatching south of Saskatoon. It was early May, but spring was only beginning. We had been walking beside a river that had cut a deep meandering gully through the soil of the prairie, the banks covered in a thick mat of bushes and low trees not yet in leaf. The afternoon had been disappointing and we had gone back to the car when I gave the bushes one final sweep with the binoculars – and there was a mountain bluebird on the topmost twig of a bush, a male in its plumage of deep royal blues, fluttering to keep its balance in a strong breeze. I will probably never see another of these stunning birds, but the memory has the assuredness of a poem that has written itself, suddenly and inexplicably, and is there before you on the page. It is both yours and nothing to do with you, a gift that you searched for and did not deserve.

I am not sure why birds especially have attracted me in this way. Out walking in the countryside, I look just as intently at insects and plants, but apart from butterflies, I have only mastered the names of a few species. I admire amateur naturalists who can identify at a glance whatever they see around them, but I have never been like that. Likewise, though I have the nine-volume *Handbook of the Birds of Europe, the Middle East and North Africa* and consult it regularly, the scientific study of birds as practised by ornithologists does not appeal to me. What I am drawn to is the aesthetics of birdlife which would be diminished if I became involved in the measuring, counting, behaviourist approach of science. This sounds Keatsian, but I do not mean that I consider ornithology a waste of time or that its findings are unimportant – I wouldn't own the *Handbook* if I thought that. My interest in birds *is* Keatsian, I suppose, in that birds have a beauty all of their own which has evolved through the diversification of species over millions of years; this beauty has, or can have, great appeal to us, even though we know it is a by-product of the way the human brain has evolved and not a function of the endlessly varied plumage of the birds, as an earlier homocentric observer might have believed.

The beautiful patterning of the plumage of, say, a goldfinch evolved incrementally over many thousands of generations, yet each goldfinch, as you watch it feeding on a thistlehead, appears exactly right; nothing, you feel, could or should be changed. The analogy with poetry is a remote one in that the processes are very different, yet a poem too, if it is successful, appears fully formed, alighting on a branch of the mind with a life of its own. It too is a product of "evolution", the evolution of the poet as a practitioner, the long hours when nothing comes, or when what emerges is malformed and has to be discarded. For the poet should be as profligate as nature; only the poem that is perfect in all its parts and which has come in Keats' phrase as "leaves to the tree", survives.

MOZART ON THE BEACH AT WAIKIKI

A television advert a few years ago showed a wind-up gramophone in a jungle clearing. The 78 rpm disc had just finished playing and the needle hissed back and forth, back and forth, in the final groove as the gramophone wound down. Someone had just left the scene, but there was no indication as to who it was – a soldier, perhaps, in the Burma campaign of the Second World War?

The gramophone reminded me of William Paley's watch. It was Paley who, in the eighteenth century, argued for God's existence from design in nature. If we were to come across a watch lying on the ground, we would know, from its intricate structure, that it must have had a designer. In the same way, he argued, the complexity that we see all around us in the natural world must have had a designer too, and that designer must have been God. *Q.E.D.*

Darwin demolished this argument, of course, in *The Origin of Species by Means of Natural Selection*, published in 1859, fifty-four years after Paley's death. In nature there is no need for a designer – natural selection, acting on variation within individuals of a species, over hundreds or even thousands of generations and millions of years, accounts for the teeming variety of life on Earth and all the intricate adaptations that deceived Paley into believing they must be the work of the Great Designer.

Yet a surprising number of people are unable to accept Darwin's refutation of Paley, as anyone who has talked with a

Jehovah's Witness or a Mormon will confirm. Perhaps, worldwide, among those who have heard of evolutionary theory, a majority refuse to believe it, preferring biblical revelation or the false logic of natural theology.

If an intelligent alien came across that gramophone, though, it would rightly deduce a designer from its structure, the materials of its component parts, and above all from the fact that the gramophone cannot reproduce itself, and thus cannot have evolved as a species in nature. The alien might perform the experiment of putting two gramophones in a cage to see what happened, but the lack of baby gramophones, or indeed of any activity whatsoever, would confirm the initial hypothesis that this was a manufactured object. The alien could legitimately wonder who the designer was.

That gramophone, with its stylus hissing in the final groove and its World War setting, is an apt metaphor for humanity. We are the intelligent species, the makers, and what we make can gladden our lives or bring us to the edge of destruction.

It also reminds us that we are, pre-eminently, a musical species. One of the most poignant of palaeoarchaeological finds is part of a bear's femur, excavated at Divje Babe Cave 1 in Slovenia. Dating from the Mousterian period, 70,000 to 32,000 years ago, it has holes punched into it at regular intervals. It may be a kind of flute, and as such the oldest musical instrument yet discovered. Certainly by the time of the Cro-Magnons, archaeological evidence for music is well established. According to Ian Tattersall in *Becoming Human: Evolution and Human Uniqueness*, early Cro-Magnon sites over 30,000 years old have yielded "multiholed bone flutes capable of producing a remarkable complexity of sound." Other sites have brought to light what may be the remains of percussion instruments, and one excavation revealed large flint blades laid out in a row, which may have been what Tattersall calls a "lithiphone", a Cro-Magnon precursor of the xylophone.

All human cultures have music, and this is so as far back as the historical record holds. One of the pleasures of life is being exposed to the great variety of musical genres and styles that have evolved around the world. And who wouldn't wish to hear the music of the Cro-Magnons, a music of flutes and drums and lithiphones that is lost to us for ever.

Only for a little over a hundred years have we had the experience of listening to the music and voices of the dead. It is true that folk tradition transmits instruments, styles, melodies and songs from generation to generation, though it is usually impossible to say how far back any one of them goes or how much has been changed in the transmission. It is also true that notation allows musicians to recreate the music of composers who lived in the last three or four centuries. In recordings, however, we hear music as it was played at the time by the musicians themselves, and in a very few recently-derived folk traditions, such as the blues, we can be certain that a tradition has been preserved on record almost from its inception.

A distinctive feature of the hominid genus is that it appears to have a high turnover of species. A medium sized species of mammal can expect to survive on average for between 5 and 10 million years. The longest surviving hominid, *Homo erectus*, existed for about 1.8 million years; the Neanderthals for approximately 130,000 years. As to *Homo sapiens*, we have been around for 200,000 years and there is no knowing, of course, how far into the future we may survive.

We are a uniquely clever species, and it is possible that we will find ways of surmounting the problems we face in the twenty-first century that have been the subject of these essays. Whether we do or not, and uniquely clever or not, the evidence of species extinction in the palaeological record suggests that at some point in the future – it may be in hundreds, or thousands, or even several hundred thousand years – our species will come to an end. When that happens, what should the music be to play us out? (The image of the wind-up gramophone comes to mind in that jungle clearing, and a hand placing on the turntable a shellac disc.)

It might be the vibrant drumming of the West African coast; an Indian raga; a New Orleans funeral band playing "Didn't He Ramble". Perhaps it should be the sombre music of Beethoven's last quartets, Bach's reflective cello suites, or the *tour de force* of Chopin's études. Each would say something about humanity.

If I were there at the end, though, I'd choose one of Mozart's divertimenti and play it on the beach at Waikiki, as the sun sets across the Pacific. And I'd follow on, if there were time, with some classic Hawaiian recordings – Sam Ku West's "Drowsy Waters", perhaps, or Charles Frederick's Hawaiians playing "Blinky Moon Bay". I might include Sol Hoopii's languorous "Na Lei o Hawaii".

Mozart would have liked Hawaiian music as it developed in the 1920s. A music of the light touch, a butterfly music of worlds that could never be, but performed by master musicians for whom nothing on their instruments was impossible. Mozart had that butterfly touch too that flies out over the abyss into which all life must fall, celebrating our transience like Sam Ku West, Charles Frederick and Sol Hoopii, and making you feel that though human life is brief, barely registering on the scale of geological time, it was worth it after all.

About the Author

John Barnie is a poet and essayist, and was the editor of *Planet, The Welsh Internationalist* from 1990-2006. John has published several volumes of poems, mixed poems and fiction, and collections of essays, one of which, *The King of Ashes*, won a Welsh Arts Council Prize for Literature in 1990. His selected poems, *Sea Lilies*, was published in 2008, and *Trouble in Heaven* (2007) was longlisted for Welsh Book of the Year.

John also plays guitar in the blues group The Delta Planes, having previously played i Llaeth Mwnci Madoc/Madoc's Moonshine,, a bilingual blues and poetry group. He was born in Abergavenny, Gwent and lived in Denmark from 1969-1982 where he taught at the University of Copenhagen.